DETERMINED

An American Journey to Purpose

Frank Tucker Ebang

Foreword

It was not until I had lived four years as a foreign student in the United States that the necessity to author this book began to haunt me strongly. It is important for everyone at a certain moment of their existence, to reflect on their life experiences and assess the impact of those events on their life's journey.

This book is the true expression of a personal adventure, the occurrences of which have left me with no other option but to sit and begin recounting those realities that have helped shape my personality, making me a man ready for any situation life might throw at me. I recall my father telling me one day that, determination is the key virtue in a man's pursuit of happiness, but it was not until I moved to the United States that I grasped the significance of his words beyond their literal expression.

In this book, one thing that I know with certainty, is that I have tried to share an episode of my life as a foreign student and a dream-chaser in the United States of America. Unveiling realities and challenges, that, although specific to my own experience were also shared by many other foreign students and immigrants in the United States of America.

I truly hope and believe that my story will serve as a model, not only to foreign students in the U.S., but also to anybody else seeking to fulfill whatever goal it is that they have set, and to understand that determination is the one key to a person's ability to bring his or her dreams to reality.

Acknowledgments

This work would not have been achieved without the help and support of the Almighty God, who remains the source of all great inspiration. I still commit my life to serving you through the effective use of all the skills and aptitudes you have bestowed upon me, so that glory be only to you. It is to all my relatives and friends stretching across the four corners of the hemisphere that I owe this publication.

To my father, Dr. Medard Toung Mve, thank you for always being my rock and support, but more importantly thank you for believing in me and being a loving father.

My mother, Micheline Nfono Tomo, I cannot thank you enough for carrying me into this life, loving me and always praying for your children. I love you.

all my siblings, I love you all and I thank you for being in my life.

To Daniel Britch Yumasi Ebang, my son, daddy loves you.

My wife and life's partner Helene Ekome Effa, you and Derek were the missing parts in my life, thank you for saying yes to becoming my partner in this life's journey, and accepting the whole of me, and not ceasing to push me to becoming the best version of myself every day. I love you.

Dailane Ntsame Toung Mve, my twin sister, only God knows the extent of the love and affection I have for you, as we both boarded the train of life to a destination known only by God.

To Vladimir Mvono Toung, my brother, for constantly being our father's presence around me after you joined me in America, I salute you.

My aunt Suzanne Ntsame Mve, I do agree with my father that you have been the hand of God that has allowed me to make it to America and begin this journey. From high school, you have always inspired and motivated me to be not only among the best in school, but also a man of faith. Thank you so much, and I hope this book reveals the esteem I have for you.

Angono Allogho Guy Patrick, a loyal friend, brother, and spiritual booster. Your repetitive reminders and suggestions about this book have helped me finish and publish it, and I hope that you find in here the expression of my true respect for the man you are.

Doris Atsu, words would not be enough to thank you for helping at a moment I felt like I was running out of resources to finalize the publishing process of this work. I pray that God finds a way to thank you enough for your support and trust at a time no one else could help me out.

Mrs. Kathleen Dahir at the English Language Institute in Libreville, I will never be able to thank you enough for your dedicated work to help Gabonese students make it through the process of coming to America.

To Mrs. Pearce, my American mother, I hope this book will make you proud as you continue to believe in me.

To all the good-hearted friends at the First Baptist Church in Sherman, Texas for the love and care you have expressed toward all the foreign students at Grayson County College. only God will be able to reward you enough.

Last but not least, my appreciation goes to the brilliant team of editors at Oliver & Theodosia Mba Editing Services for the work and insights provided to produce this book.

To everyone else in my life I love you all, and I am grateful to count you as parts of my life's journey. I hope this book makes you all proud.

Contents

Introduction

Few months following my graduation at Paul Indjendjet Gondjout High School with a baccalaureate degree in literature and languages, I was awarded a government scholarship to continue my studies abroad. A formal admission letter from an accredited academic institution at the school of my choice was the condition for the scholarship to be awarded. Aware of the requirement, months prior to graduation, I had applied to universities in Europe, particularly in France, where I hoped to be easily accepted for admission. Indeed, France was a convenient choice, primarily because of the language, but also, because I knew about relatives, and friends who had immigrated to France. Unfortunately, by the time I graduated, I still had received no responses from any of the schools I had hoped to be admitted to. I began to run out of time to meet all the requirements that kept my scholarship award in a pending-status.

Aunt Suzanne, who, was my English instructor during my sophomore year, had talked to me about the possibility of going to America to continue my education after I graduated from high school. She believed that I could do well, studying in America, essentially because I could learn English fast, and thus, might not struggle to adapt with life in the United States. While teaching at Paul Indjendjet Gondjout high school, she often traveled to New York City, and would not hesitate to share her feelings about this city with the class. I often listened, and stared at her with admiration, hoping that one day she would take me with her to New York. Disappointed, and desperate for not being able to find a school in Europe, I decided to reach out to Aunt Suzanne, who had already returned to New York City. She was my last option, as I began to foresee a year at the local university in Libreville, a not- so pleasant experience, witnessing friends, struggle to validate their academic

1

years because of regular strikes that would turn into major riots opposing students and the police. Luckily for me, it did not take long, before Aunt Suzanne returned my calls, following failed attempts I made to ring her number in New York City. She advised that I make sure to translate all my high school transcripts, and diploma to apply to schools in the United States. Because I knew of no translators in Libreville that could do the task, she recommended that I go meet a man named Mr. Nguema, who would translate the documents for me, at a reasonable rate for me. Mr. Nguema oversaw the English department at the Ministry of Education. The man spoke and knew English like a British reporter. I was dazzled by his deep voice, and how well he could articulate, with no accent as he talked to me. Within a couple of days, following our initial meeting, Mr. Nguema had translated my transcripts, and notarized all the copies as required.

For a while, after my documents were ready, I was unable to get back in touch with Aunt Suzanne. I attempted to reach out to her by calling the number I had of her in New York City but could not reach her. As days passed, I obviously grew frustrated and desperate, I began to believe that it was not meant for me to go to America. While hoping to soon hear from Aunt Susanne, I decided one evening to start looking for schools online, but I needed to have access to a computer, and the internet, and it was then that Mrs. Kathleen Dahir became a major character in my adventure to America. I had met with her years before, when I was the chair of the Martin Luther King, Jr. English club, which was a mini structure attached to the English department at Gondjout High School. Years before I started high school, a group of students, eager about learning the English language, started to meet up after classes, to discuss subjects in English, and ended up starting the Martin Luther King, Jr. English club. All members of the club were required to study, and master the civil rights movements, and its most iconic figures. We held special days to commemorate the life and achievements of people like Rosa Parks, Dr. King, Malcolm X,

Black scholars such as W.E.B. Du Bois, Booker T. Washington, and many more.

Mrs. Dahir worked as an attaché to the U.S. Embassy in Gabon, and she had lived in the country for years. She understood well how the country worked and what the realities were for students struggling to succeed. She taught English at the country's main university in Libreville, the capital city of Gabon. She also ran her own English language institute not too far from the campus where she taught. Her institute had an up-to-date library of English and American literature, which far exceeded the country's main university's library. So many students would go to her institute for private courses, to conduct research for their classes, to have access to better materials, or to have a fun time in a nicely updated library. She also would host major events and celebrations of U.S. holidays, and the embassy's officials would go there and hold lectures or seminars on major subjects of U.S. history and academic opportunities. University students were required to attend those events, and at times, they would send invitations to the MLK English Club to attend those lectures.

The English department often rented a bus to take every student active at the Club to those activities at Mrs. Dahir's institute, which in most cases, were broadcasted on national television channels. Parents were proud to watch their children on TV attending events hosted by U.S. officials, especially as everyone interacted in English. Those were good moments filled with fun experiences and adventures for high school students in Gabon. The experience of the MLK English Club played a key role in my life as a student as well as a man. It was only years later that I would look back and realize how much good the Club had done for me.

I decided to go to the English Language Institute to meet with Mrs. Dahir, hoping that she could help me identify schools in America. But I had no idea that it was actually a part of her business at the institute, assisting students and families with planning to continue their education in America. In fact, Mrs. Dahir leveraged her connections in the States, to recommend good schools in America, and facilitate the admission process for international students. She understood the Visa process at the embassy and would help students with the application process all the way through the interview. Recalling the few occasions, I had met her, while hosting English events with my friends at the Martin Luther King, Jr. English club, I hoped she would be able to recognize me, and accept to help with my situation at a lower fee.

Mrs. Dahir was the embodiment of a busy body; she never had a moment alone in her office. As I walked in along the hallway leading to her office, I watched people in and out, mostly parents seeking her services for their children planning to pursue their studies in America. She was as fluent in French as she was in her native English, so she had no problems talking to anyone who visited her office. I thought, if I could speak to her in English, it might help her recall about the Martin Luther King, Jr. English club, and hopefully, facilitate our interaction in that regard.

When she invited me to enter her office, after I had been waiting in a hallway leading to her office, I immediately greeted her in English and began a conversation just in English with her. She stared at me for a moment and began to laugh, while everyone else in the room stared at me, dazzled, and surprised with my fluency in Shakespeare's language. She asked where and how I had learned to speak so fluently. I told her that I was the chairperson of the Martin Luther King, Jr. English Club during my senior year at Gondjout High School. Nodding, she recalled about the club, and smiled. I smiled back to her, reassured that she could recall about the club and our various initiatives to promote the English language. As she reviewed my transcripts, and other documents in the folder I handed over to her, Mrs. Dahir confirmed that it was all that I needed to begin to apply to schools in America. She, then told me that, I needed only to provide the fees for her to mail the documents to the

States, to a couple of schools she represented, and wait for them to respond. She said it would take days after they have received my documents to reply. I rushed home that day and told my father about my visit to Mrs. Dahir's office. He gave me the money to cover the mailing fees, and I returned to Mrs. Dahir with the money so she could start the process for me. After a few days that same week, I received a call from Mrs. Dahir, and she informed me that I was admitted to an English program at Mount St. Vincent College in Riverdale, New York. The joy was so intense, I hurried to get to her office as soon as she hung up. The next day, I went for my Visa interview at the U.S. Embassy and got it that same day in the afternoon. I was ready to go to America. It was like being in a dream I did not want to wake up from. I look back to how I managed to make that happen despite obstacles and roadblocks I encountered while trying to find a school abroad. Somehow, the power of determination was beginning to set the course of my life.

The night I left, all my siblings and closest relatives joined my parents at the airport. There was a mixture joy, and sadness, as I was going to a land none of them had been before, a place they had all learned about, mostly the news on TV or through movies. Everyone had something to say to me about never changing my identity, or forgetting about where I came from, as I live in America. There were talks about life in America, as if they knew for certain what it was like over there. But I knew they all wished me well, and hoped strongly that I would make them proud. By the time the announcement was made that people departing to America had to head toward the security-check room, my father held me aside, looking at me straight in the eyes, and with his low and calm voice, he said, "Education is a race, and from here, you have proven yourself to be able to win that race". As I am your father, I see no reasons for you not to do well in school. Now, you are going to race in the land of giants, and you would need to become one, for you to win the race."

That night, my father suddenly sounded like someone who knew something about where I was going but did not want to tell me and hoped only that I would find out on my own once in America. With a flow of emotion in my mind, staring at my father and all my brothers and sisters waving goodbye, I could not ask my father what he meant, but I promised him that I was going to remain focused on the purpose I was leaving for and honorably carry his name, which he always said was his one legacy to all his children.

Early Days in America "New York City"

Leaving my home country, my family, and all the people I had lived with and shared important moments of my childhood, was not an easy decision to make, but I needed to do so for the love I had for them all. I understood that at a defining moment in life, a man needed to make sacrifices to reach his goals and fulfill his ambitions.

Although in the plane, I knew for certain that I was bound for America, I did not realize so until we landed at JFK International Airport in New York City. I kept thinking that somehow, it was all a dream and that soon, I would wake up. How was it that I really was going to America? I began recalling all I knew and had heard about the States from Aunt Suzanne and from news on TV channels.

I just could not stop thinking of the fun times spent back home with my friends and family. At one point, it even felt as if I was not going to see any of them anymore. I recalled the moments of fun I spent with my friends at the MLK English Club, imagining us in a U.S. city, sharing drinks with unknown taste, hanging here and there with beautiful movie-like American women. I thought about how fortunate I was to be one among my friends to go to America while we all shared the same dream. The mentioning of cities such as Las Vegas, Los Angeles, Miami, and Atlanta used to put a smile on our innocent faces, as we could only imagine those cities.

Now sitting alone on that plane, I kept wondering about the reasons behind my fascination for America, at that decision I've made to leave behind my family and the people I have known for a long time behind. Everything happened so fast that I began to think that it was too good to be true for me. I looked around and I saw an old white lady who had not taken her eyes off her magazine from the time we boarded the plane until then. Was I the only one in that plane who was going to America for the first time? It seemed so, as everyone else appeared so comfortable and relaxed.

After hours in the air, one of the flight attendants announced that everyone needed to buckle their seatbelts and adjust for landing. I felt like I was being brutally woke from a long sleep. I clicked in my seatbelt and stretched my legs forward to make sure I was ready for the landing at JFK International Airport. As the plane began to descend, I felt my eyes widely opening, the tension creeping over me. No doubt, I was scared and stressed out by the whole landing experience. Then it was done, and I could hear the plane's tires hitting the ground, and all of the sudden, everyone in the plane began to put their hands together, clapping with joy and congratulating the pilot for his safe landing. I had never seen that before, for the time I could recall flying in a plane as a child back home. It was so nice and new to me, seeing all those people joining their hands together for the pilot. Eventually, I ended up doing the same. That was it, and I was in the United States of America.

"Welcome to JFK International Airport, and the captain wishes you a nice stay in New York City, and again, thank you for boarding Morocco Airline." The voice of the flight attendant was soft and friendly and stole a smile from all the passengers as people rushed up from their seats to grab their carried-on luggage, getting ready to exit the plane.

I kept hearing people around me calling New York City the Big Apple, and I wondered what it meant and why the Big Apple. So, when I exited the plane, I asked the flight attendant helping people out of the plane, why they called New York the Big Apple. She smiled and told me she really did not know, but surely, I was going to find out by the time I was in the city. We both laughed about it and I thanked her for the service and kindness during the flight, as she was the one who often came to check on me.

As I walked through the hall leading to the terminal where everyone else was heading, I kept reminding myself of how important it was to watch over everything I carried with me from the airplane. My father had insisted that I be careful with my things as I arrive in New York. There were two lines formed as we walked into the terminal. One was for U.S. citizens and permanent residents, and the other was for people on Visas. I eventually figured out which line I needed to follow, making sure to pull out my documents, passport, and Visa paperwork handy. After standing a few minutes behind a gentleman who was being checked in by the immigration officer at the gate, I was asked to move forward and show my documents. I had never in my life seen a man as tall as that immigration officer. He had dreadlocks as long as those I watched, growing up, on TV reggae musicians. I have always enjoyed reggae as a music genre, and Rastafarianism as a belief system. His uniform was well-stretched and aligned with his body posture, and the sight of his gun and other accessories scared me a little bit. But the man smiled at me and asked how I enjoyed the flight. I told him that I had a great flight, although it was too long . He smiled again as he opened my passport and went on flipping pages to reach the one that had the Visa stamp.

"There it is. I see that it is your first Visa ever!" the man said after he found the page with my Visa number.

"Yes, sir, I have never left my country before."

He smiled again and asked if I was excited about coming to America. I told him that I could not even express how excited I was. I even told him that I still thought I was dreaming. He did not say anything after that but stapled a little card with a set of numbers in one of the pages of my passport. Then he told me to keep that card in my passport during my entire stay in the U.S. – this was the document that proved that I entered the country legally.

"Again, welcome to the United States, and I wish you good luck with your studies, Frank."

"Thank you so much, sir, and yes, I am happy to come to America."

He handed my documents back to me, and I safely arranged them in my handbag as I walked past the gate where I watched people walking from every corner, taxi drivers and men holding cardboards with names written in grand characters. Certainly, they came to pick up newcomers who had arranged to be picked up, I guessed. I needed to find my luggage first. I asked one lady who shared the flight with me, where was it that we are supposed to get our stuff. She pointed to a corner not too far from where we stood and told me, "Yea, it is right there! I am heading there, too, to grab my luggage."

"Thank you, I need to get my bags, too."

We both walked to the place she pointed, and she was right. I saw the old white lady with her magazine in the plane during the entire flight, and I said hello to her. She greeted me and threw a smile back at me. I smiled back and walked forward to get my luggage.

After I picked up my luggage, I began to think about how to contact Aunt Suzanne. I had her number; my father had advised calling her as soon as I arrived at JFK. I needed to find a phone to do so. There happened to be a public phone in one corner not too far from where I was standing. I walked to the phone and dialed the number for Aunt Suzanne.

"Hello, hello, Aunt Suzanne! It is me, Frank. I am at JFK right now. We just landed, and I already finished gathering all my luggage with me."

For a moment, the phone buzzed, and I barely could hear what she was saying. Then, everything cleared up and I could hear Aunt Suzanne laughing over the phone.

"Hey, the American guy! I am happy to hear that you are over here now. Well, I am still at work for the moment, but I am almost done.

Just wait for me there and please do not go with anybody else. Understood?"

"Sure, Aunt Suzanne, I will be waiting until you get here."

Then the phone stopped, and I could no longer hear her. I thought I had run out of money to carry on the conversation. So, I looked for a place to go sit while waiting for Aunt Suzanne to come pick me up.

After about two hours of waiting there for Aunt Suzanne, she still was nowhere in sight. I began to wonder if she still will make it to the airport. I knew that she would not leave me at the airport like that, but the fatigue was getting to me, and I began to feel very exhausted. But just when I wanted to stand up and walk to the restroom to freshen up hoping to feel less sleepy, I felt a hand on my shoulder, and when I turned to find out who was touching me, I saw Aunt Suzanne standing before me.

I cannot explain how happy I felt to see her. I had not seen her for a long time, and there she was in front of me, in the United States of America.

"How are you doing, young man?" she asked with a smiling face.

"Well, yes, I am doing incredibly good, Aunt Suzanne. I am so happy to see you again. In fact, I was beginning to wonder if you had forgotten about me."

"No, I couldn't have forgotten about you. I just got caught into the traffic on my way here. The traffic is always that way when you come to JFK, especially days like this."

Aunt Suzanne had not changed a bit from how I remembered her. She still looked the same from her days at Gondjout High School as one of the most feared English teachers there. I recalled the times she would brag about me being her favorite English student. The smile on her face made me feel so comfortable, and we both stood

11

there for a moment, talking about my flight and how my parents were doing back home. Aunt Suzanne had not been able to contact my father, after they last met before she moved to New York, so she asked about him and about my mother too.

As it was beginning to get late, and most people were rushing out of the airport to get a taxi and get to their homes and places, Aunt Suzanne suggested that we leave too. I grabbed my luggage, and she helped me carry the two carried-on bags that were less heavy as we exited the airport main lobby heading toward the taxis outside. I could not hide how stupefied I felt, as we stepped out and I had my eyes on the tall and beautiful buildings facing the airport.

"My goodness! I have never seen such tall buildings."

"Of course not, young man! You have lived your entire life in Gabon, and surely our country is not even close to having buildings as tall as those," she said with an expression that told me I had yet to see amazing things in New York City.

"You are absolutely right, Aunt Suzanne. This is more than amazing."

"Well, wait till we go to Manhattan, and especially in Times Square or Grand Central." She talked about those places that I did not know about, and I could only look forward to visiting them.

"Well, Aunt Suzanne, I am really in America now, and I cannot wait to see it all."

We got into a yellow cab, and Aunt Suzanne told the man to take us to Harlem and precisely on 125 street. I only heard people saying addresses like that in movies, and here I was in New York City, enjoying a yellow-cab ride. We drove past nice-looking, tall buildings and supercenters. Everything was so huge that I could not help keeping my mouth wide open with fascination at the sight of such marvels. Aunt Suzanne kept smiling and mocking my behavior in the cab.

"Look at you, Frank! You are just like someone waking up from a long dream. This country is really going to take you out of your mind, young man."

I could not say anything to her but kept looking around all the streets we drove through. It really was a hell of an experience for me. I only wished my friends at the Club could have been with me there and felt what I was feeling in that cab. Then, we arrived in Harlem. I had read about Harlem in the many history books I'd checked out at Mrs. Dahir's library. I learned that Harlem was the heart of the African Americans' community in the United States. It was the place where every Black man in America, during the times of rough oppression on people of color, wanted to move for a better life. I also read about the Harlem Renaissance, as Harlem produced the greatest African American scholars in the history of America. Poets, painters, and musicians of unique styles enjoyed the stages of Harlem. There I was, in Harlem. I thought about Dr. Martin Luther King, Jr., Rosa Parks, and Malcolm X, as we used to study those characters at the Club.

"Here is the place I surely can identify with as a Black man in America," I said to myself as the cab driver opened the trunk for us to get our stuff.

"Welcome to Harlem, young man!" Aunt Suzanne said.

I smiled and pulled my bags out of the trunk. Then I asked the man how much the fare cost. He told me that I needed to pay forty dollars. Although I still did not have good knowledge of the dollar currency, I was able to give the man the right amount of money before saying thank you and followed Aunt Suzanne into the building in front of us.

All those buildings looked the same from the outside. Our building number was twenty-seven east, and Aunt Suzanne insisted that I remember that number because at times, I would be on my own as she would be working by the time I return from school. I needed to remember the number to not get lost or confused by the buildings. We walked up to the second floor, and there, was the room. She opened and entered first as I waited for her to invite me in.

"This is the place, young man!" she said.

"It is a nice place, Aunt Suzanne."

"Yea, I believe that for a start, it would be okay for the two of us. I am still looking for something bigger than this. But it is so hard to find a pretty decent place these days in Harlem."

The room was a studio – which included a set corner for the kitchen, with a dishwasher included. On one side by the window, there was a single bed which I figured was Aunt Suzanne's. Then there was a couch, which she told me was convertible to a bunk bed. Then, she proceeded to show me how to convert the couch to a bed, as it was going to be my bed for the time. After I managed to find a spot to gather my luggage in one corner of the room, I told Aunt Suzanne that I was tired, but before I could fall asleep, I needed to call home and tell my father that I had made it safely to New York. I knew everyone back home certainly was waiting for that phone call. She told me there was a convenience store just on the other side of the building, and that I should go there to purchase a phone card that would allow me to call home. I rushed down the stairs, back to the main entrance, and walked to the store she had indicated. As I walked to the convenience store, I looked around me and saw real Americans, just like on TV with NYC Yankee hats, and huge colorful jackets. Some of the men had dreadlocks, just as long as the ones the immigration officer at the airport had. Others had their hair completely and nicely braided, with shinning earrings, and golden chains as necklace. All of this looked very cool to me, and I imagined I would soon embrace that New yorker style. It all seemed so normal, and nobody felt any type of way about men with braided hair and earrings, something not so well admired in my home country.

"I am really in America!" I reminded myself.

I now was walking in the land of the free, a country where everyone understood what it meant to be a free man and live your life as you felt like. I got into the store and asked the cashier for a phone card to call Africa. He grabbed a card from one of the shelves behind the register and told me it cost five dollars. I pulled out my wallet and handed him a five-dollar bill, feeling proud that I was now using the American dollar.

After I returned to the room, I dialed the number and my father picked up the phone. "Hello, Dad! It is Frank. I made it safe to New York, and I am with Aunt Suzanne now."

"Thank God! I was in fact waiting for you to call, because I figured that you should have been there already. How is Suzanne doing?"

"She is doing all right, Dad! Hold on a second. I am going to give her the phone so you could talk to her." I waved at Aunt Suzanne as she stood at the kitchen, trying to fix something for dinner.

I handed her the phone and she talked to my father for a good while as I sat on the couch, trying to unpack my things. Then Aunt Suzanne handed the phone back to me so that I could continue the conversation with my dad. We continued to talk about my flight, and I told my father how long of a flight it was. We laughed about it for a while, and he advised that I rest before I did anything else because my body certainly needed it for me to feel better later. I told him that I would call him the next day before Aunt Suzanne and I could go to the school for my registration. I could tell that my father was exhausted; I called at a time he normally would have been asleep, not minding the six hours' time difference between Gabon and the United States.

After the conversation with my father, I decided to lie down on the couch and do nothing else as Aunt Suzanne was fixing dinner. My eyes scanning the room; I noticed the English books, on English Literature, French and English dictionaries. Aunt Suzanne had majored in American Literature and received her bachelor's degree in France before she decided to return to Gabon to teach English. She was the kind of lady who showed exceptional love for the things she did. At the time, she was teaching English at Gondjout High School, she had gained the reputation of one of the most demanding professors on the campus. They were students would not hesitate to switch classes as soon as they found out she was going to be their teacher, because they knew she was not playing with her homework and tasks load. I, on the contrary, had always enjoyed language classes regardless of who the teacher was going to be.

Students even nicknamed Aunt Suzanne, "the iron lady" because of her tough character, especially when a student was being lazy during her class. I personally was excited about having her as an instructor. I loved to have tough instructors because it was an opportunity to distinguish myself through my hard work and prove that I was among the best students in the entire school. Plus, I loved English, and Aunt Suzanne was going to help me improve my speaking because she spoke only English during her entire class, and most students could not stand it. My friends who knew my passion for languages would hurry to propose to be my seatmate, as students sat in pairs in most schools of the country. Sometimes it would be an opportunity for me to choose one who was good in math and sciences because I did not do well in those subjects.

Aunt Suzanne would enter the classroom and order everybody to stand up and begin to introduce themselves in English. It was a nightmare for students for whom English was not a favorite course. They just had not realized at that time the necessity for them to learn

English. Aunt Suzanne would often question the academic level of a student when he or she was not able to say their name in English.

"My goodness! I cannot understand how, at this level of education, you all are incapable of saying your name in English," she would shout.

I personally enjoyed the moments when she was upset with those students who could not say words in English because I knew she would call for me to speak and set the example for my classmates to follow. I also knew that not all my classmates were fine with that. There were students who thought that she did it on purpose just to present me as her favorite student. But I did not really mind what my classmates thought because I knew that I loved English and wanted to be the best at it. Sometimes, Aunt Suzanne would smile a little when I forced an American accent, which often left my classmates overly impressed. They thought that I really sounded like an American.

I believed that Aunt Suzanne, too, was somehow impressed with the passion I had for English. Sometimes she would send for me in her other classes when students were not able to solve elementary grammar issues. I still remember the time students believed that I was Aunt Suzanne's son, and therefore it was normal for me to pick up English like I did.

They were not wrong about that because it finally came to be that Aunt Suzanne, who until then, I considered just my English instructor, was related to my father, as they came from the same ethnic clan, the Effack people, one of the largest groups in the northern province of Gabon, which, according to tradition, made the two of them relatives. It made me feel at home to be in New York City with her then.

After we finished eating dinner, I began to open my luggage one after the other, taking out clothes that I was going to wear on a regular basis for school. Aunt Suzanne sat on her bed where she was finishing paperwork. One other thing that I noticed about Aunt Suzanne that night was that she was a highly organized person who always made sure everything is where it was supposed to be. It was not too easy of a task for me, though, as I had not always been a highly organized person and my bedroom back home was often a mess. My father did not like it at all, and I remembered him telling me that even if a man was poor, and did not have possessions, he should always be clean and organized with the little he has. I would stand there, listening to him lecture me about keeping my room organized.

While trying to organize my clothes and make sure I had everything I would need for school, I began to feel homesick, especially after I pulled out a photo, I had taken at the airport that night with sisters prior to boarding the plane.

"Are you all right young man?" Aunt Suzanne asked. She stared at me and could see the sad expression on my face. "Are you homesick already?"

Of course, I was homesick already, and I just did not know how to hide that. They were so far from me, and I knew it would be a long time before I could see them again. For a moment, I lost my excitement, making room for an emotional moment, taking me back to my family. Images of those moments in high school with my friends began to flood my mind. I could not help but recall the simple life in my village, where I would go to my grandmother's plantation and just sit there, eating bananas, sucking dry sugarcane while she was busy with whatever she worked on. The sad emotion would come back and haunt my thoughts, taking away the joy of being in America.

"You will be all right soon!" Aunt Suzanne said, smiling.

She sounded like she knew exactly what she was talking about. I supposed she must have felt the same when she first came to America.

"Once you begin classes, all these emotions will go away, and you will be fine."

She was right, but I still could not keep myself from feeling bad about it. It was almost dark outside and the street was increasingly empty and noiseless. I stepped over to the window to look and I could see that there were still people out there. Again, I wished all my friends from the Club were there with me to share the wonderful experience I was beginning to have. Then, it was time for me to go to bed. Aunt Suzanne was already asleep, and I did not want to make too much noise and disturb her sleep, so I converted the couch to the bed before I covered it up with my blankets and lay down to sleep.

The next day, I woke up too early and Aunt Suzanne thought that it was not healthy for one who had spent so many hours on a plane. The truth of the matter was I had always been a morning person. Plus, my father hated it when any of his boys stayed in bed too long. He often said that a man is supposed to be the last to go to bed and the first to get up from bed. He himself was the perfect example of what he taught us.

Aunt Suzanne had already taken her shower and seemed ready to begin her day. I just could not remain in the apartment, and moreover, it was my second day in New York City. I needed to go outside and see things. Aunt Suzanne talked about Times Square and Manhattan while we were in the cab coming from JFK. I wanted to see what they looked like. I was excited that morning.

All the tenants of each floor shared a bathroom, and therefore it was important to wake up early to not have to wait in line. I finished taking my shower and dressed for the day. Aunt Suzanne told me that we were going to the school because she looked over my documents and, I was late for class by a day. I needed to go introduce myself so the school can keep me registered for the session. Aunt Suzanne told me that the school was on the other side of the Bronx, in Riverdale, and that we needed to catch the Number One train and a bus to get there. It was a Monday morning in New York City and the traffic was going to be intense as everyone headed to work and different activities. We left the building and walked to 125th heading to the nearest subway station, which was on Lenox Avenue, a couple of blocks from our place. While walking toward the subway station, I felt like I was coming out of nowhere. Everything was so nice, even the air I breathed seemed different from the air back home. People dressed very nicely in Harlem. It was all about style and fashion. I looked at Aunt Suzanne that morning and she, too had gotten into that Harlem vibe. She walked fast and I barely could keep up with her.

"In New York, you must be fast, young man!" she said, as we got closer to the subway station.

She was indeed right about everyone walking fast and even talking fast in New York. Although I had a basic knowledge of English, I just could not get what all those people were saying around me. It made me feel like a child who could not speak at all. I surely was beginning to feel what my classmates felt during those English classes with Aunt Suzanne at Gondjout High.

I was impressed by the height of Harlem's apartment buildings, which you could see on each side of the street Aunt Suzanne and I walked on.

"You can now see what life is like in the U.S., young man, and I really hope you get to fit in because there are going to be times when you will have to walk here on your own."

We walked down into the subway station, and Aunt Suzanne told me to wait on one side as she was going to get me a metro card that would allow me to pass the gate and board the train. I had never been to a metro before, and being underground that day, I realized that there was another life going on atop us; this was magic to me.

How did men build something like this? I asked myself while looking around every corner in the station.

Aunt Suzanne handed me a yellow card with blue lines all over it and told me it was my metro card and that I could use it for a whole month before I needed to get another one. The card allowed me to take the trains and ride buses, too. We both slid our cards at the gate and walked to the other side of the station where everyone else stood, waiting for the train to show up. It did not take long for the train to arrive, and everyone rushed to get in. Aunt Suzanne and I stepped into one of the cars and managed to get an empty seat while so many people had to stay on their feet.

"Stand clear the closing door please!"

I did not know where the voice came from, but it sounded so good to listen to it at every station we stopped. It was a woman's voice, though, and I first asked Aunt Suzanne what it said because I could not understand the whole expression. Aunt Suzanne told me to listen carefully and practice my listening. After a couple of stops, I finally could understand what the voice was saying.

"Stand clear the closing door please!"

It asked that people step away from the doors when they were closing. I wanted to pass my first English test that morning on the train. We arrived at our stop after about fifteen minutes of riding the Number One train. Aunt Suzanne held my shoulder and told me that we needed to step out of the train. Then we walked about a hundred feet from the train station and took a bus that Aunt Suzanne told me was taking us straight to my school. While on the bus, I noticed that most people carried backpacks, read their books, and others listened to music through their iPods or other electronic devices I had never seen before. I figured out that they were students heading to their campuses.

After another fifteen minutes of riding, Aunt Suzanne requested the stop and we exited the bus. Mount Saint Vincent College was on the other side of the street. We walked straight toward the campus's main gate. There was a security guard who asked to see our IDs before we could go forward. Aunt Suzanne pulled out her ID card and handed it to the man while explaining to him that I was coming in to register as a new student and that only after I was registered could I have a proper identification card. The man looked at Aunt Suzanne's card and returned it back to her; then he opened the gate and we walked in. It was a pretty huge campus, and as Aunt Suzanne and I walked toward the admission office, I wondered if I one day would be able to walk in there by myself. We passed through both a basketball court and a football field, where I could see college students sitting on the grass with books all around them.

I recalled those days at Gondjout High, with my friends, studying for a test or engaging in debates related to a topic we discussed during class. It seemed so familiar to me that I began to feel homesick again. Aunt Suzanne was already far ahead of me as she continued to ask about the way to the administration building. Finally, we arrived in front of a huge red brick building. Aunt Suzanne looked back at me and asked that I hurry because she was going to leave me there and head to her job. I did not get what she meant by leaving me all by myself at that campus. One lady wearing blue jeans and an orange shirt approached us and asked if we needed any help. Aunt Suzanne explained to the lady that I needed to register for the ESL program. She smiled and told Aunt Suzanne that she was Rebecca, the one in charge of meeting with new students who came for the ESL program. Then she asked that we both follow her to her office. We got into another elevator that took us to the second floor of the building where Rebecca's office was. As we walked into her office, she asked that we be seated while she looked for my file.

"What is your last name, Frank?" she asked.

"It is Ebang Toung Mve."

"Thank you, Frank. I got it just right here."

Then she pulled the file with my whole name on it and set it on her desk.

"So how was your flight, Frank?"

"It was a long one, but it was all right. The pilot was good," I said with a smile on my face.

"Have you had any English before, Frank?"

"Yes, I did take years of English when I was in high school, and in fact, my aunt right here was my English instructor." I looked over Aunt Suzanne and we both smiled after I responded to Rebecca.

"That is great! I can in fact see that you are fluent for a non-native. I can predict that you are going to do well with your classes here because it is all basic notions, which I suppose you already know."

I indeed felt extremely comfortable speaking with Rebecca. I understood well everything she talked to me about. Her English seemed so clear to me that I did not need her to repeat anything. She later told me to feel free to look around the building as she entered my information in the school's system. It sounded fine to me because Aunt Suzanne was ready to leave, too. She had to rush to her job, so she told me not to worry about making it home by myself because it was quite easy, she said. I needed to catch the same bus we took from the train stop and do everything backwards until I reached 125th Street. Then she left and I walked to the lobby down from Rebecca's office. It was a large room with chairs all over, with tables for those who had something to eat or drink while reading their lessons. I noticed that there were Asians in the room. I could not tell if they were Chinese, Japanese, or Taiwanese because they all looked alike to me. I decided to go take a seat next to everyone else so that I did not look too new in school, although I was. After few moments, one of them walked up to me and began to introduce himself.

"Hey! My name is Tomohiro and I am from Japan," the young man said.

"Hello Tomohiro. I am Frank and I am from Gabon."

"Nice to meet you, Frank. You can call me Tom. That is how everyone else calls me here," he said.

"Okay, Tom. It is good to meet you and I really hope we get to know each other better."

Tom was a tall guy with Asian's eyes. He had long hair, which set him apart from the rest in the room. I had seen Japanese people before, but he had something unique because he was an open person and everyone else seemed to have a good relationship with him. After about thirty minutes, Rebecca came over and asked that I follow her.

"Well, Frank, I have everything all situated for you, which means that you are ready to begin your classes with everyone else. I also see that you already have met your classmates."

"Yes, I have met some of them, I guess, and I think we are going to get along."

"Oh, sure you will. I like all these kids, and you have pretty fun instructors, too."

"Good, then I am really going to enjoy my time here."

Rebecca and I laughed for a while, and then I told her I needed to head back home. She handed me my schedule for the entire session there and I left. While on my way back to Harlem, I kept reminding myself that everything was going to be all right and that I was not going to get lost. I waited for the bus, just as Aunt Suzanne had indicated. It did not take too long before the bus arrived. We reached the train station, and I could make it to the Number One train, which took me to 125th street.

It felt so good to reach Harlem. I recognized the buildings Aunt Suzanne and I had walked by earlier and therefore was able to make it back to our building. Aunt Suzanne returned home late, and I remembered that we did not even talk about each other's day because I was already in bed, and she was exhausted from working the entire day. Later the next day, she asked if I had any trouble while returning to Harlem. I told her everything was fine and easy to follow. It was another day then, and we both left the apartment at the same time for different destinations. I took the train to Riverdale, and she headed to her job. Harlem seemed more familiar to me on that day. I had begun to grow accustomed to the neighborhood. Nothing was too new for me anymore as I took the ride for a couple more days by myself on my way to school. Aunt Suzanne even asked that I meet her someplace, and I could do so without too many difficulties. I recall that I had begun to view myself as a native of Harlem when asked where I came from by fellow students at school.

My first day of class was just as exciting as I had expected it would be. I attended my first class with Mr. JM, as he told the class to call him. He introduced the class to listening competencies. We listened to conversations in English and were asked to tell what we could catch from whatever we heard during the conversations. The assignments we had with JM were not too new to me because I had already taken listening classes back home at the Club and at Mrs. Dahir's institute. It was not the case for my fellow students who were Asians. There were students who used translator devices to be able to effectively get all that was being discussed in class. I had never seen those devices before, so I clearly was stupefied.

After the class with JM, we all gathered in the lobby and discussed how each one of us enjoyed his or her time out of school. Rebecca joined us that morning and asked how I was enjoying my classes. I told her everything was going all right and that my classmates and I were having fun times in class, especially with JM, who turned out to be a very funny and smart instructor. Rebecca agreed that JM was one of the best instructors for the program I was enrolled in. She told me she was happy that I was having an enjoyable moment with my classes and my fellow students. Then she asked me to meet her at her office after I was done talking with my friends, which I did right after she walked back to her office.

"I wanted to let you have this document which outlines the tuition charges of your session. In fact, the director of admissions informed me this morning that you have not made your payment. I thought by the time we first met that it was already submitted like the rest of the students on scholarships."

I did not understand what she was talking about because I thought that my scholarship had been transferred to the school as it was arranged with the office in charge of it from Gabon. Then I realized, as Rebecca made it clear to me, that something was not right and that I needed to check that out. So, I told Rebecca that I was going to take care of that the next day and that I needed to speak with my parents about it. She heard me and did not make a big deal of the issue; instead, she told me to continue to have fun with my fellow students. Nevertheless, this situation left me somehow embarrassed, as I could not believe that my tuition had not been covered by the scholarship I was granted. As I walked my way out of the campus, I met with Tomohori, who suggested that I join the rest of the group for lunch at the school's cafeteria. Because I realized that I had not paid my tuition yet, I did not want to go to the cafeteria that one could have access to only after having paid tuition. I told Tomohiro that I did not have enough money to pay for my meal at the cafeteria. Again, he looked at me with a big smile and told me not to worry about it because he was going to take care of it for me. I thanked my Japanese friend and promised to pay him back as soon as I received the money from my scholarship, which I believed was not going to take too long. But I guess, I was completely wrong about that. Tomohiro insisted that I did not have to pay him back and that I would hurt his feelings by doing so. I felt somehow warmed up by Tomohiro and his easy attitude, which kept surprising me. Of course, I am not saying that Asians did not get along with Africans; I just had not befriended an Asian before. But from what I heard about them not opening to non-Asians and enjoying only their own community, I had not expected this from one of them. I was now learning about the weakness of stereotyping. It is so amazing how life or nature will teach us through living experiences, helping mold our personality. During my early days in the U.S., I first befriended a Japanese student who was proving to be open to that friendship. As we headed to the cafeteria, which was not too far from the admission office, I asked Tomohiro how long he had been studying at this campus and what he was going to do when the session was over.

Sometimes, I could not understand my friend very well because of the strong Japanese accent he had. But I often managed to let him know when I understood him well. I figured out that it was a part of what I needed to do to encourage him to speak and enjoy conversations in English. Plus, JM told us during class that we needed to talk to each other in English, even when out of classes, because it would help us discover unfamiliar words and improve our vocabulary. So, I found it interesting that Tomohiro would speak English with me, contrary to most of his other friends, who spoke only Japanese. They would smile at me when I said hello or hi to them. My friend Tomohiro would keep smiling at them, sometimes saying something in Japanese and then coming back to English, laughing a little, while putting some tomatoes onto his plate to go along with his salad, as I would be waiting for a waiter to pick a burger for me. I surely loved being around those guys even though

I felt lost and confused when they began speaking only Japanese. I picked on Tomohiro sometimes to remind him that I wanted to be a part of the talk and would not mind at all some other times.

The cafeteria at Mont Saint Vincent College was a very cool place, especially because it was not only a place to eat for international students, but for all students who attended the college. As foreign students, we benefited from the many opportunities to befriend American students and practice our English. By the time, I returned home that day, I had in mind that I needed to call my father to tell him about my talk with Ms. Rebecca and make sure he dealt with my scholarship. I stopped at a grocery store on 125th street a block away from the famous Apollo Theater in Harlem.

Sometimes, I took pleasure in walking the streets in Harlem, enjoying the opened-air performances of various artists, from painters, singers, dancers, up to young men and women engaging in rap-battles. All of it, reminded me of Mont Bouet, the largest marketplace in Libreville. People rushing from every street corner, some selling their goods, merchants pilling their items, shouting the discounted prices for the first customer. I really enjoyed going there with my friends after classes, just to have a fun time.

When I made it home, I decided to call my father right away, though I worried about having to wake him up at that hour of the night over there. After the phone rang about three times, he finally picked up. He sounded very tired, so I knew that I woke him. I told him I was sorry for that, but I needed to tell him about the money issue I had discussed with Rebecca. He explained to me that I needed to take Aunt Suzanne with me to the school and she would take care of it as she already had one part of the money, he had sent to her for my tuition and that he was going to send more via Western Union. I thanked Dad and once again apologized for the late call. Before he hung up, he asked how I was feeling and if I liked the place we stayed at. I assured him that I was all right, and the place was fine, too. I did not want him to worry about anything else but my school tuition, which in fact was the only issue as of then. We said good-bye to one another and ended the conversation. After talking with my father, I felt a lot better and was relieved. My father had always had that special effect on me every time we talked, and he would always uplift my spirit and boost my sense of self-esteem and confidence. I remember one day we were both engaged in a discussion about the things I wanted to do in my life, and of everything I said, he always told me that he, being my father, did not see anything that would prevent me from succeeding, if I really wanted to go for it. I always looked at him as my personal spiritual guide, a confident who would always say the right thing at the right moment to calm me down.

Aunt Suzanne returned from her job, and this time we could talk and ask about each other's day. She still looked exhausted, but better than the night before. I told her about the tuition issue at school and my conversation with my father.

"Okay, remind me of it tomorrow so I can give you the money before you leave for school and you can take care of it with Rebecca," she said after I told her everything.

"Great! I surely would remind you tomorrow, Aunt Suzanne."

Aunt Suzanne brought home a cake and told me it was mine because she had already had enough from her job. I got up, served myself, and began to enjoy the sweet chocolate cake. The next day, I headed to school, but made sure to call my father again so he would give me the information I needed to go cash the money he had sent via Western Union. Fortunately for me, the phone did not have to ring even twice before he picked up. He gave me the transfer number and all that I needed to go cash the money and complete what I had to do to have my tuition paid. Before we ended the conversation, I asked my father about my scholarship, and he explained to me that he was heading to the bureau in charge of that and I would need to call him back later in the day to find out what they had told him.

Once at school, I walked to Rebecca's office, and by the time she saw me coming, she gave me that big smile she carried the first day I met with her.

"Good morning, Frank! How are you today? Are you ready for another day with JM?"

"Good morning, Rebecca! I am fine, and yes, I am excited about today's class with JM. I wanted to first take care of my payment as we discussed yesterday."

"Yea! Great, we surely can do it right away, Frank, and you can go enjoy your class. I just need to pull out your folder and get some information, and that is all."

She stepped over her chair and grabbed a pile of folders with names on the top of every one of them. These were some sort of archives or records of all students who attended the school. She finally picked one that she set on her desk before she sat down again.

"Here we go! This is your folder, and it contains your application and all the documents we received from Ms. Dahir in Gabon by the time she applied for us to send you an I-20. Now, you just need to sign some of these documents for me to complete your folder and get the money so you can head to class."

She printed two documents that looked to me like financial proof, attesting that I was going to take care of my living expenses and tuition during the session of classes that would last a month. The other document was an admission letter that recognized me as an official student at the ESL School of Language at Mont Saint Vincent College. I gave her the money, which she counted first before she put it in an envelope that she deposited in a brown wooden box on her table.

"Now you are ready to go, Frank! This is your receipt to keep for your records in case you need it, and see me whenever you need anything, okay?"

"Sure, Ms. Rebecca! Have a good day as well."

I left her office and walked to my class. I was surprised, once there, to be one of the first students in there. I looked for my friend Tomohiro, but he, too, was not there yet. I exited the room again and went by the lobby and curiously found that they all were in there. I felt a little bit confused and asked if we were not having class today. Tomohiro explained to me that we were in fact having class but not in that room for the day because it was a computer class so we all were waiting for another teacher to take us to the computer room. This looked more like a long break for me because the other instructor did not show up after about an hour and we just spent time together in the lobby, talking from one group to another. I would admit that it did us some good because we could get to know each other better as we shared stories about where we came from and looked for similarities. I seemed to be the one with a quite different story, as most of the students in the room were Asians and knew each other from having attended previous sessions of classes together. I noticed that they would all come and gather by my friend Tomohiro and me to hear about Africa and ask about things they had heard about as far as the continent was concerned. The computer class was something new for me. I had not had a computer class before, and although I felt excited about getting to learn about computers, I also felt a little bad because I would look at all the Japanese and Chinese students, typing so fast with eyes off the keyboard, while I sat there, trying to figure out where each letter was. Tom Jeffrey, the computer class-instructor, would always come over to my desk and make sure I was doing well. I would look at him and let him know that quite frankly, I was struggling with my typing speed, and he would laugh a little before explaining to me that it was a matter of habit, and that the more I used the keyboard, the faster I would become. When I was in Gabon, I had already been in contact with computers, but I would say that it was more about knowing how to create an email. That was the basic knowledge I had about computers, and therefore, the idea of a computer class was so interesting to me that I spent

31

most of my after-class hours in the computer room, trying to work on the things Tom taught during class. I wanted to be able, by the end of the session, to type on the keyboard as fast as most of my classmates did. Sometimes I would ask my friend Tomohiro to sit with me and start a typing race to see who could type a sentence faster than the other, and I would admit that Tomohiro won every time we did it. Somehow, I did not feel uncomfortable or down with him being faster than me on the keyboard; I just learned that I needed to spend more time on the keyboard than I had been. I needed to be able to know where every letter was and locate it without having to look at it. That was how my friend Tomohiro and the rest of my classmates did it. I promised myself I would reach that speed someday, and no matter what it took, I was going to be able to use a computer keyboard as easily as my Asian friends. That day, after class with Tom was over and I was done with my lunch at the cafeteria, I headed straight to bus station because I wanted to catch the very first bus to stop by. When I got home, I found that Aunt Suzanne had already returned from her job.

"Hello, Aunt Suzanne! Is everything all, right?"

"Hey! What up? I am doing fine."

She did not look exhausted, and it did not seem all right to me because she always looked tired when she returned from her job. I could feel that something was going on and I needed to know what the matter was. So, I did not restrain myself from asking.

"Why are you home this early, Aunt Suzanne?"

She sat there on her bed, which was covered with clothes that usually would be in her bags. I also noticed that she had been shopping.

"I am going to Gabon next week young man. I need to go deal with some family affairs over there and supervise some of my construction work in the village."

After she said it like that, I calmly sat on my bed and began deeply thinking about what I had just heard. I did not even know what to begin thinking and how to think about it. What I knew for sure is that I was beginning to feel uncomfortable, like someone who had been told the worst of the news. What was I going to do all by myself in this city? I just got here and knew nobody else but Aunt Suzanne. Did she think about that? Somehow, I was scared and did not know how to tell Aunt Suzanne about my concern. I decided not to say anything and hoped that she would figure that out. We ended up that night sleeping without adding words or talking about her travel. I did not have class the next day because it was the weekend. I decided to just stay in bed. Aunt Suzanne got up early, took her shower, and left the room. I could see her rushing that morning while I was still in bed, making sure all my body was well covered as it had begun to get cold out there. The winter was approaching and it was beginning to be cold in most places. Thinking about it would make me wish we already were in December so I could see snow for the first time ever. I wanted to see it and touch it for real. This was an experience I had watched people explain on TV shows and say how happy they felt the first time they touched it. I also would say that it scared me because I did not know if I could stand that kind of freezing weather. It already was getting painful for me to have to double most of the clothes every time I went out, and Aunt Suzanne always reminded me to get my jacket when she saw me going out, even when I was only going on the other side of the street to purchase a phone card. She always told me how this weather was going to deceive me and make me run home for a jacket someday. Sometimes I would look at people on the street and they would look funny with their big hats, long scarves, and jackets that I believed weighed twice the weight of those who wore them. No doubt, every guy I met on the street had a strange walk, as if they had something on their back. I soon understood that they had to dress like that to be able to stay on the street for long hours without having to complain about the cold. For a minute, I stood by the room's only window, which gave us a pleasant view of the street, and from there I could feel the fresh air.

The loud voices in the street and cars passing by created a more vivid image of the whole neighborhood. I decided that I would stay home that day and read while enjoying Harlem's fresh air in my room. I did not want to go out at all or getting to see something new that day. Moreover, I thought that Aunt Suzanne might come home early and need me for something, as she knew I did not have class that day. When in the room by myself, I would begin reading one of Aunt's Suzanne many books she kept on top of a desk she bought months before I arrived. Somehow it felt good to just be there in the room and enjoy that solitary moment. I had picked a book titled *Huckleberry,* and the author was Mark Twain. I had never read a book by that author before, but I knew about Huckleberry being Thomas Sawyer's best friend. It is at that moment I realized that what I had watched as a cartoon back home in my primary school days was a written story by Mark Twain, and that discovery made me want to read more about the author. I would go pages after pages, trying to capture every single detail of Huckleberry's story. I wanted to somehow recall parts of the many episodes of the cartoon by reading the book. But by the time I was beginning to deepen my reading, a sound pulled me back to the room, and it was the phone ringing. When I picked up, it was Aunt Suzanne's voice, and she asked if I could meet her by the closest train station on 125th and Lenox because she wanted us to go meet some people from Gabon, as they needed to meet with me. This was good news for me, especially because Aunt Suzanne was about to leave the States. I needed to meet people who I could spend time together with after Aunt Suzanne left. I grabbed a shirt from the closet and put on jeans before heading downstairs in a rush to meet with Aunt Suzanne. The

Lenox train station was about one block from where we stayed; therefore, it did not take me too long to get to the station and begin looking for Aunt Suzanne.

"Hello! Young man!"

"Hey, Aunt Suzanne! I was just looking after you and beginning to wonder if I was at the right station."

"Yea, you got it right. I was just trying to get myself another Metro card, as this one is running out of credits."

"So where are we going?"

We need to go to 144th Street and Amsterdam. I want you to meet a friend of mine. His name is Emile. I told him you were coming before you even got here so he wanted to meet you, and as I know that his place is home for every Gabonese, you certainly will get to meet with some other young guys like you who go to school here."

"Well, that sounds good to me, especially as you are leaving soon. I would need to hang out with some people to not be by myself all the time."

"I know, Frank, and it is especially because of that that I thought you should meet them. Otherwise, I would not really suggest that you meet them."

We got on the other side of the subway to catch the coming train which was to take us to 145th street and Amsterdam Avenue so that we could walk down to 144th and Amsterdam. It was a fast ride about one station-stop before we reached our destination. I had never been to that side of the city. Aunt Suzanne told me we were in the Bronx and that mainly Hispanics lived in that part of the Bronx. In fact, as we walked down to 144th Street, I could hear Spanish from the sidewalk. Aunt Suzanne added that, that part of the Bronx was home for Puerto Ricans, Dominicans, and some Mexicans. That mix of minorities from all races, and ethnic groups in one place is the essence of the *American melting pot*, a concept I remembered from my history class in high school. Looking around me, I felt at home, and because I could also speak Spanish surprisingly good, I wanted to engage with everyone on that street who spoke Spanish. I do not think Aunt Suzanne knew that I was fluent in Spanish, until I decided to greet one of the guys standing by a grocery store, which looked familiar to me, as it resembled the place, I went to buy my phone cards, to call home. As I approached the man, I began speaking in Spanish to him, and as we carried the talk, I saw Aunt Suzanne's face, unable to hide her shock, and after I said good-bye to the man, she put her arm on my shoulder and asked where I had learned to speak like that. I laughed for a while, and then I told her I learned Spanish back home in high school and that I was an active member of San Jose de Calasanz Spanish Club at Gondjout High School. Aunt Suzanne was so impressed then, she just looked at me and asked that we hurry to cross the street.

"There it is, right in that red-bricked building, but we need to ring so somebody can open the door for us from there."

The building looked new, at least compared to where we stayed, even though I found the neighborhood too noisy and somehow unsafe. While we stood there in front of the door, and Aunt Suzanne pushed the ringing button, I saw someone looking down at us from an open window on the top of the building. I told Aunt Suzanne, and she nodded as to let me know that she knew someone was coming. After about a minute, I saw a man coming to the door, and as he unlocked it for us to enter, Aunt Suzanne began laughing at him. I could feel how familiar this was to me. For a moment, I felt like I was back home and just visiting an old friend. The man smiled at me and introduced himself as Emile, and holding the door open, he invited me to enter.

"You certainly must be Frank Tucker, the Gabonese American!"

"Yes, I am Frank Tucker. Nice to meet you, Emile."

"Nice to meet you, too, Frank. You are so welcome. This is your place, so just make yourself at ease," he said, pointing at a seat for me.

"Thank you so much. I am really pleased to meet you, as I was beginning to wonder if there were any Gabonese in this New York City."

We walked upstairs and entered a room that opened toward a huge white fridge, on the side of which stood a small table with a TV on top. The room looked very Gabonese, and what I mean by that is that I could really feel home at first sight. There was a stony sculpture from the Mbigou stone of Gabon on one corner of the table and pictures of Gabonese cities hung on the entering wall. Two other guys sat there on chairs across from a white plastic desk with beers on each side. One of them stood up and introduced himself to me.

"Hello, I am Nzamba, and it is good to meet you."

"Hello, Nzamba. I am Frank Tucker, and nice to meet you as well."

The other guy finished the drink he held before stepping over to my side and introducing himself.

"Hi, man. I am Doctor Mba and you are welcome to this place, Frank. Your aunt told us about you, and we all were expecting you."

Everybody appeared so nice to me, and I related to the atmosphere. The music in the room was Gabon, and deeply in myself, I planned to be there all night.

Emile went to the fridge and asked what I wanted to drink. Before I even said anything, one the guys in the room, Nzamba, loudly responded, "How can you ask such a question, Emile? The guy is a Gabonese, and what it means is that you just get him a beer and he would know what to do with it."

It sounded funny to me and to everyone else in the room. Nzamba was certainly right about me wanting a beer, but it was out of the question for me to drink a beer before Aunt Suzanne. I just could not do that. So, I asked if he had an orange juice or a soda. Emile interrupted before I could even finish pronouncing the word soda. "Well, you do not have to be shy, Frank. We all know you all drink, and just do not worry about Aunt Suzanne. I am telling you; she knows."

I laughed at that but insisted that I get a soda. He grabbed a Coke from the fridge and handed it to me. I thanked him and popped open the can.

"So, what is new back home? We always ask the new-coming people to tell us how the country's going."

I looked at Aunt Suzanne, who before I even said anything, responded by asking Emile if he expected any change in Gabon. I knew what she meant by that because I knew that Aunt Suzanne, as well as many Gabonese victims of the long-time-established system, had lost hope of any change in the country if Mr. Bongo remained in power. Aunt Suzanne was a qualified English teacher who received her bachelor's degree in English from a well-renowned university in France. After she graduated, she thought she needed to return home and contribute to the country's development by teaching English to Gabonese students, as many other teachers did. For the many years, she served as a teacher, however, the Government was not able to pay her what she deserved for a prolonged period of time. She had to live through odd jobs and personal services she provided to individuals who needed to learn English. So, the system broke her, and once she had the opportunity to leave the country, she seized it and now was working on her own profit, trying to maintain a certain status in her family and high esteem for her person. Emile certainly knew about it as he also left Gabon in the search of better opportunities to make up his life. I then understood that asking about things in Gabon was somehow ironic and I shared the irony.

"You know your country, Emile. Things are still hanging, and then the same sufferings and same joys," Aunt Suzanne said. "The Gabonese people have learned how to cope with the system."

I did not really want to reveal my personal position about the system, even though I did share Aunt Suzanne's belief. We stayed there for about an hour, talking about anything, laughing at Emile's very funny adventure, as he recounted for me his story of arriving in the States. I had never heard such a story before, and I admitted that at a moment, I felt the pain in Emile's voice while telling us his story. He had lived in Gabon in demanding situations, as he did not have enough financial means to provide for his basic needs. He struggled, as I knew many did in Gabon and in most parts of the African continent. But he had his idea and it was to save as much money as he could to be able to leave the country and head to America, the land of the all-possible and the last hope for a struggling individual who believed in a better tomorrow. When he could purchase his ticket and provide for most of the documents required at the U.S. Embassy for a Visa, he boarded a plane to New York, where he arrived in the very cold month of December. Emile had never imagined a place could be that cold. He did not know anybody in New York. Moreover, he did not speak any English at all. Nor did he know Spanish, and to add to problems, he did not have any money left for him to even have something to eat. All that he had saved was used to provide for his airplane ticket, and now he did not have money. So, he spent three days at JFK International Airport, sleeping on benches, hoping someone would come help. The third day, as passengers arrived from a flight coming from Morocco, he decided to help a man who struggled to carry his luggage out to a taxi. The man, while thanking him, asked where he was from, and Emile told the man he was from Gabon and had just arrived at the States. The man was choked up from hearing Emile's story so he decided to take him with him so they could look for the Gabonese Consul in New York. It was like God's response to Emile's prayers, and as they both boarded a taxi, Emile thanked the man. While closing the cab's door, he looked up into the sky, and with a move of his. head, he thanked God. The man certainly had been to the States before and he knew New York City and how to locate the Gabonese representation in the city. After a short drive, they stopped by a hotel and the man walked in to ask a receptionist for an address book to look up the address for the Gabonese consulate. When he found it, they both went back into the cab, and he asked the driver to take them to the consulate for Emile to meet Gabonese officials there and see how they could help him. The more Emile continued with the story, the more I got very emotional, as I hardly could remain indifferent to the story. They reached their destination and the man asked for the cab driver to wait for them as they went into a glass building. After they passed through a huge revolving door, a concierge welcomed them and asked if he could be of help. The man with Emile explained to the concierge that he needed to go to the Gabonese Consulate. The other looked at him with a confused expression before he told them that the Embassy of Gabon was in Washington, DC but only the Gabonese representation to the United Nations was on the third floor of the building. Emile's good Samaritan told the man it would be fine and that they were looking for that very office. Then they got to an elevator, and when they reached the third floor and Emile saw the Gabonese flag, he hurried to get in and before an attendant could talk to him, he grabbed his good Samaritan in his arms and thanked him for all he had done for him and that now he was home. The man smiled at Emile and before returning to the elevator, he told Emile to do the same to someone else and that would be the best way for him to thank him. Emile promised the man to do so and wished him all the best during his trip in New York. Now, Emile reached that part of his story, I almost shed tears and deeply in myself, thanked God for having allowed me to know Aunt Suzanne. Unlike Emile, I could have someone take care of me when I entered the United States.

Emile got up from his seat and walked to the fridge, where he grabbed another beer for himself while we all sat there trying to bring our awareness back to the room. I could see that Emile's account of his story took us all to another world – a world of compassion, I would say, as no one could have heard such a story and remain indifferent to what happened to Emile, especially as we all had come from the same country and could relate to Emile's reality. I had never been abroad before, so this whole situation was not only shocking to me, but also scary because I was beginning to see the reality of people who were victims of an unjust government. I mean, if while in Gabon, Emile could provide for the basics of his life and self-improvement, as a few of the Gabonese elite did, he would not have taken the risk of traveling to America with no money and no idea of what it would take for him to live in America. He only knew that he needed to get out of this place where none of his dreams could come true. I personally came to America to continue my education and return home when finished with it, but here was a grown-up man who had a professional life in Gabon, someone who struggled with the many injustices of the system and decided that he would not deal with it anymore; therefore, no matter what the price he had to pay, Emile chose to leave.

It was getting late, so Aunt Suzanne asked if I was ready to leave. I responded that I was ready whenever she wanted to go. So, we both got up from where we were sitting, and while she was teasing Emile about the many drinks, he had had that night, I walked by the two others to say good-bye. They told me they looked forward to seeing me soon, and maybe we could share a drink sometime. We all laughed at that, and by the time I walked by Emile, he smiled at me again, and holding his beer can in his right hand, he hit me on the shoulder with the other hand and repeated to me that I was welcome at his place and that when Aunt Suzanne left, I could come over anytime I wanted to. I thanked Emile and promised that I would be back soon.

Aunt Suzanne and I left the room and walked down the stairs to exit the building so we could go look for a taxi, as she suggested that we do because it was too late and she did not trust taxis at some hours of the night. It was easy to get a taxi from that area; as Aunt Suzanne and I walked along 144th Street, a black Lincoln stopped and asked where we were headed. Aunt Suzanne responded that we were headed to 125th Street and Madison. The man told her he could take us there for eight dollars, and Aunt Suzanne agreed. While in the cab, I began to ask myself why such a nice vehicle served as taxi, when back in Gabon, this would be the property of some important personality. The only answer I could get was that I was now in New York City and no longer in Gabon. I wished I soon would begin to feel as relaxed with all this as Aunt Suzanne. It was quite impossible to know when she was impressed with the things around her, and I would sometimes feel like I had lived for a long time in a cave or somewhere that did not give me any idea how pleasant things could be in other places. We got home safely that night, and Aunt Suzanne reminded me to not sleep too tight because I had class tomorrow, and I would not want to wake up late the next morning. I was in my early days in New York City, and I was beginning to feel as if I had lived there for a while. Certainly, the routine of going to school from one side of the city to another was making me feel like that. I barely called home to ask about my siblings, and when I did, it would be just for a couple of minutes. We all were beginning to accept the reality that I was going to be away for a while and it would do me good to avoid calling home all the time; instead, I should stay focused on the things I had going for me in the States. Aunt Suzanne was ready to leave for Gabon, and I was almost done with my first session at Mount Saint Vincent College. I had been informed at school that by the end of the session, I would have to make another payment equal to my first one to remain enrolled in that school, or I could transfer to another school. Two days before Aunt Suzanne left, we both sat in the room and she asked how I thought I was doing so far. I told her I felt like I was okay and that I was feeling more comfortable with life in New York City. She stared silently at me for a while, then asked if I was sure that I was having a good relationship with life in New York City. I did not know what she was getting at, but I responded that was doing fine. Aunt Suzanne stood up and walked to the window, and from there, she told me that she was happy for me and knew that I would do just fine when I arrived, but she stopped for a minute and added that I needed to nevertheless to start really paying attention to how things worked around me. I asked her to narrow it down for me so I could get what she meant. I did not even finish asking, and she told me that I needed to begin thinking about getting a job because she was leaving and would not be able to pay for the room's rent while in Gabon. At first, I did not understand what she meant by saying that I needed to get a job, but when she added that she would not be able to pay for the rent, then it began to light up in my mind and suddenly I felt as though I had brusquely awakened from a long sleep. In fact, I had never thought that we had to pay rent to anybody because the room in my mind belonged to Aunt Suzanne, and the notion I had was that Aunt Suzanne certainly bought the place and therefore we were all fine to live there. Now, it looked different to me, and I needed in fact to come back to Earth and play by the true rules of life abroad. Aunt Suzanne walked back to her bed and continued talking to me, adding that I needed to help my dad and the only way for me to do that was to find a job so I did not have to call and ask him to send money to me whenever I needed it. Moreover, she added that I was not the only one my parents had to take care of, and because of my siblings back home, I needed to begin taking care of myself just as many other kids she knew who were in my situation. I truly felt lost for a moment before I realized that she was right and that it was time for me to be more independent from my family. I never did something like that before because I had always counted on my parents for everything I needed and my father was always making sure that I had what I needed to focus on my studies and not have to worry about anything. Aunt Suzanne shook her head to let me know that she really was serious about it and hoped that I would think about it. I told her I would do something about it but needed to tell my father about it so he would not be surprised to hear me asking for some rent money. I knew myself that it was the right thing to do for my father to not to have to do something he did not expect. Aunt Suzanne agreed with that and before she lay down on her bed, she asked about the school and what I was going to do once the session was over. I told her I did not know yet but certainly would talk with my father to see what he thought I should do. Then, she asked if I had heard anything about my scholarship since the last time, we talked about it. I could not even answer that one because I did not know what was going on with it. I decided not to say anything, and she got it and knew that things were not right about it. The following day, I got out early so I could get to the grocery store across the street to purchase a phone card to reach my father and find out about my scholarship. After the phone rang twice, he answered and asked if everything was all right. I told my father things were fine but I needed to hear more about the scholarship issue because my session at the ESL language school was over, and I needed to know if he wanted me to stay there or look for another school. My father, with his never-disturbed voice, told me he was going to meet the people in charge of my case and see what was going on because they promised to give him a call at their last meeting but never did. He tried to assure me I should relax and not worry about it because things would be fine and we always found a way. I believed my father but at the same time, I felt a bit of doubt in his belief that I was going to get that scholarship. Well, I said to myself that if God allowed me to arrive in the United States, certainly he would make sure everything turned out to my advantage. My father asked about Aunt Suzanne, and I informed him that she was going to be there soon and I was going to live by myself for a while. He did not seem to find any reason for me to worry about that and even reminded me that if I were able to live on my own during my senior year in high school, he believed I would be okay. He was right about that and while on the phone, I laughed at him and assured him I was going to be fine. Before we hung up, I asked about my twin sister, and he informed me she was doing fine but busy in her studies. He finally asked me to call him back the next day so we could find out about the scholarship and how I was going to manage with school. That day, I decided to walk out on 125th Street with finding a job in mind. Aunt Suzanne left for the day as well but told me she was not going to stay out for long, as she needed to have most of her things packed because she was leaving the coming week. I thought I needed to begin looking for something, at least to experience what it was like to look for a job in New York City. The idea was somehow funny to me because I did not imagine I would need to do that anytime soon. But I agreed with Aunt Suzanne that I needed to help my father and can provide for some of my basic needs by myself. While walking up and down along 125th Street and Lenox, I decided to stop at Burger King and ask if they needed anybody for any position available. A beautiful young lady with a Burger King T-shirt and a black cap welcomed me at the door and asked if she could help me somehow. I told the lady I needed a job and hoped they had an opening. She gave me a big smile and added that they were not hiring at that time, but I surely could fill out an application. I agreed to do so and left the place after I got done. Then, I did not believe I was going to get anything that day, so I walked in and out from different clothing stores, trying some out and walking the street, looking at tourists who were taking pictures of anything that was presented to them. I thought of myself as more of a guy from Harlem than an African student. Somehow, I was getting acquainted with the neighborhood, even with those guys along the street vending their products and enjoying the pleasant atmosphere of that area of the Apollo Theatre. When I returned home, Aunt Suzanne was already back and had cooked some chicken mixed in a tomato sauce just the way I liked it. I hurried to have some of it before she began telling me about her day. We stayed there talking about anything and laughing about Emile's story, as she brought it up again.

The week that followed, I went back to Riverdale and spent good times with my teachers and all my friends. But it also was the last week of the session, and we were all asked to make sure we talked with Miss Rebecca about our plan so she knew who was staying and who was leaving. I asked my friend Tomohiro what he was going to do. He told me he was taking a break for that session and was going to travel to Europe. I asked him where he was going, and he told me he was going to stop in Paris, then Milan in Italy, and Spain before coming back to New York. I was really impressed with that and did not mind asking him what that was for and how he was going to pay for all that. As usual, he gave me his big mocking smile before he told me that he was paying for it and that he already had everything taken care of but needed to take his finals before he could take off. I understood that we came from two different worlds and that he certainly belonged to a well-off family who could help him afford those expenses for the sake of having fun and discovering. I told my friend I did not know what I was going to do, but certainly would stay if my scholarship were ready, but could not remain in that school with no scholarship because it was going to be too expensive for my father to afford. He looked at me with a serious expression on his face. I had never seen my friend appearing that serious. Then, he put his arm on my shoulder and told me he believed everything was going to work out fine for me. I looked at him as well and told him I hoped so and that no matter how things turned out, I would love for us to stay connected. He agreed and suggested that we have a drink at the cafeteria with the others and hear from them as well. I was finishing my first month in New York City, and it was now mid-October; I had arrived in the state in mid-September. The climate was changing as we entered Fall and approached Winter. I felt increasingly cold, and I began to limit my time outside, as I did not really like that type of weather. The last day of the session, I had to take an exam that determined every student's level for the next session, and it was going to be about all we had learned during the three weeks of classes. We all gathered in one of the classrooms, and JM brought with him a pile of exam sheets that he handed to every one of us, making sure we all understood what to do with them. I felt confident, as I always did in any exam that I took. I knew there was not going to be anything different from all we discussed about in class, and as I already was doing well there, I felt more relaxed than some of my classmates. We had about two hours to get finished with the exam and return the copies. I was done with mine after the first hour, and I was asked to have a seat in the lobby and wait for everyone to get finished so the teachers could grade the papers and hand each of us the certificate of attendance that we needed to register for the next session of another school. While in the lobby, I met Rebecca and she asked how I did on the exam; I told her I was confident. She smiled and told me she knew I would be okay and moreover, she believed I was ready for college level. Well, I did not know what to say to that, but certainly I felt like I needed something more challenging, and if college level could give it to me, then I was ready for college level. Before she walked her way back to her office, she asked if I were staying for the next session, but I told her I did not know yet, but surely would tell her after I heard from my father. She agreed and left. After a couple of minutes, more students began to join me in the lobby, and I knew time was up. Everyone was asked to leave the room. My friend Tomohiro joined me where I stood, and together we discussed what we missed so we could have an idea of what our grades were going to be. I told my friend that I was confident and that I did well so I was not really worrying about what the grade was going to be. Tomohiro did not actually look like he was even interested in the whole thing. It was as if he did not even care, and good or bad, he still was going to be there. While we all stood there, asking each other about the exam, JM came in and asked that we all follow him back to the room so we could get our grades and certificate. Tomohiro whispered to me that this was going to be fun; I asked why he thought so. He responded that he loved it because we got to take pictures and share a cake with all the teachers because we were leaving. I told him it would certainly be a fun time. JM and many other teachers lined up by the blackboard in front of all of us, and he began by thanking all the students for having allowed them to teach us what they knew about English and making sure we all would soon go to college and study for our different academic majors in the many colleges and universities in the country. After his speech, we all applauded and thanked the teachers as well. Rebecca entered the room with the certificates and told us to wait for our names to be called. We would be handed a certificate of language and a report of our grades. I loved the moment and felt happy, especially because I knew that when hearing JM's speech.

We, all had done well on the exam, so we could have fun and enjoy the cake.

Rebecca began handing certificates to each student, and when she called my name, I walked proudly toward her to receive mine and before I could return to my place, she suggested that I take a picture with her. I agreed and while we stood for the picture, I told her I would miss her and would love to be back for the next session. She gave me that sweet smile of hers and with her arm over my shoulder, she told me she would love to see me back for the next session as well, but added that no matter what, she was glad to have met me. We stayed in that room for another hour after everyone was given his certificate. It was a time for us to say good-bye to each other and exchange numbers and email addresses so we could stay connected no matter what direction each of us took. I felt a little sad when my friend Tomohiro insisted that I email him no matter what. I promised him that I would email him and would look forward to seeing pictures of him in Europe. He laughed at that and promised he would send me pictures from every city he was going to visit. Then we both separated and I walked my way out to catch my bus.

It felt quite chilly outside and I could feel the wind blowing above trees, causing the leaves to fall. Squirrels ran from every side of the courtyard and they looked so cute to me that I stopped for a while and just stared at them playing around and seeking something to eat. School was over, and it did not look any different to me from what I felt back home at the end of the academic year. My friends and I would spend time together on the campus, taking pictures at different corners of the court, remembering the good times during classes, and laughing at the jokes of some of our teachers. I was now feeling homesick by recalling those instances, but I really could not help it now, for everything seemed so similar. A good friend of mine named Waldrys would always produce a plan to keep everyone from leaving unhappily. He would suggest that we go for a drink at some of the many local pubs in Libreville and from there, we would have fun, enjoying the music and meeting with other schoolmates who had the same idea. Late in the afternoon, everyone would return home and wish to meet again the next academic year. Experiencing those moments in New York City was not too different, and even though I barely spent time with my classmates there, I still began to miss them.

When I arrived home, I grabbed the phone to call my father to find out about my scholarship and what I was going to do for school. My father was waiting for me to call so it did not take long for him to pick up and respond. I first told him that the session was over and that I received a certificate of language that would allow me to go to another school at an advanced level. He congratulated me and asked for Aunt Suzanne. As I did not find her home yet, I told my father she was not there and certainly would be home soon. Then, I decided to ask about the scholarship and before I even brought it up, he cut me off and told me he did not believe those people were going to give me the scholarship. I did not understand what was going on, so I asked that he explained what he meant and what we were going to do. He told me he went to meet with the one of the secretaries of the director in charge of the allocation of scholarships and they barely could receive him. He tried to explain his reason for being there, but still, no one could take care of him; he decided to leave the office because he knew that for some reason, they were trying to play with him as they did with many other parents he met in that office who had complained about the administration's attitude. I began to feel very frustrated and upset about it so I asked Dad what he was thinking about doing. He calmly demanded that I remain confident and faithful in God because he would always provide a solution, and he was going to deal with it. I did not know what to say because I began to realize that things were not going to be the way I thought they were. I knew that my father was going to find a way for me to go to school, but I also knew that he was going to financially hurt himself for me. I knew it was going to become difficult for everyone else at home because they all relied on my father's modest income.

I began to feel incredibly sad over the phone and I could not stop asking myself why this was happening to me. But my father assured me that I need not worry about anything else but my studies, and he was going to do what needed to be done for me to succeed. Before we stopped the conversation, he suggested that I begin looking for another school of language, especially one that was cheaper than the one I was leaving. I agreed with that, so I told him I would talk to Aunt Suzanne and certainly we could find a cheaper school in New York City.

After that conversation with my father, I decided to call Emile, as I could get his phone number the last time we met. I felt like I needed to do something fast and as Aunt Suzanne was not home yet, I decided to go meet with Emile and discuss the issue with him. I knew that he could help me locate a cheaper school in the Manhattan area and if not, he certainly knew somebody who could help me with that. He agreed over the phone and asked that I meet him at his place because he wanted me to meet with another Gabonese student who rented a room in the same building and was attending a school of language in the Manhattan area. I hurried to get there, and when I arrived, the room was so noisy, with loud music, people talking and drinking and just having a fun time. Emile's place really was home for every Gabonese, and I was not surprised to later discover that he had been chosen to be the President of the Gabonese Association of New York. The man was so cool and open to everyone who came to meet him, and he was always ready to share a beer and have a good time. I did not know what Emile did for living, but I could swear that he was happy with what he did and did not have to worry about anything. So as soon as I got into the room, all the guys in there began shouting: "Hey! Here is the fresh guy! How are you doing, brother, and welcome home, man!"

I felt warmed up within myself, and for a moment, I even forgot what brought me to Emile's place. It was as if something had been removed from me and let me be free of any worries. I joined the guys, and we all sat around a round wooden table already filled with empty and unopened cans of beer. One of the guys, who looked younger than everyone else in the room and close to my generation, put his arm over my shoulder and introduced himself as Jean Noel. I told him I was Frank Tucker. The guy laughed at that and he asked if that really was my first name or if I had made it up. I laughed as well but assured him Frank Tucker was my first name and just as he, I did not know the mystery behind my parents giving me such a name. Everyone else in the room laughed, and we continued drinking and talking about things back home and how each of us regarded the political situation of the country. While enjoying the moment, we began talking about the education system and the many injustices of which some students were victims. I decided to ask if any of the guys knew a cheap school of language in the Manhattan area. They all pointed at Jean Noel, letting me know that he was the right person to see for something like that. I then turned to him and asked what he could tell me about it. Jean Noel asked if I came to the States via Mrs. Dahir's program. I told him I had and that she had sent me to a school of language in Riverdale where I studied for a one-month session but found it awfully expensive. He agreed and told me he did not make it there through Mrs. Dahir, but he knew many of his colleagues who did. However, he went to a school of language in downtown Manhattan and that school was affordable for everyone. He added that the school may even be twice less expensive than ESL. This was the news for me, and I told him I needed to transfer and would love for us to meet anytime in the week to figure out what the process was for me to transfer to that school. He agreed with the idea and right after that, as I felt so happy to hear that from Jean Noel, I opened another can of beer that I drank with all enjoyment. Emile looked at me and began to laugh so loudly that we all looked at him with a confused expression.

"What's going on, Emile?" I asked him as we stopped.

"Well, I am just laughing at you, boy. The other day, I asked that you drink something, but you refused and made it sound to me that you never drink at all, and now I can see you enjoying that beer just as an old drinker."

I laughed at that myself and I told him I could not drink any alcohol because of my aunt, and even though she might have known that I drank, I could not do it in front of her. He agreed with me and just added that it was very funny. Everyone was having fun and I was having fun as well. As it began to get darker outside, I told everyone that I was going to make my way home because I did not want to stay out late, especially after I had had those drinks. Emile proposed to walk me downstairs, which I accepted. I said good-bye to Jean Noel and the others, promising to meet them soon. Emile asked if I needed a taxi, but I told him I was going to take the bus, as my MTA card still had credits. We waited for the bus and when it got there, I got in and Emile returned to his apartment.

Aunt Suzanne was already home when I arrived there. I did not want to talk about anything because I could not talk with her while intoxicated. So, I put myself together by the time I reached the room because I did not want her to see that I had been drinking.

"Hello, Aunt Sue! How is it going?" I tried to play fine.

"Hey! I am just exhausted. As you know, I am leaving this weekend, so I needed to purchase some things for my mother. You look tired! How is it going?"

"Well, I am tired and I have been walking outside, trying to look for a job before I went to Emile's place."

"How's Emile doing? I bet the room was filled with all the Gabonese of New York again!"

"That is true, Aunt Suzanne. I met with Jean Noel and other guys that were pretty interesting as well."

"That is good! But you must remember that I do not want you to spend much time with people from home because you need to improve your English – and hanging with them, I do not think you all would speak English."

Aunt Suzanne was right and I could only tell her that I got her point and considered what she meant. She later added that she did not mean that I should not befriend people from my country, but I should be careful who I spent time with and what we talked about. I could feel my father's words in Aunt Suzanne's warning. I fell asleep after that and stayed in bed until the next day. I needed to meet with Jean Noel and go to the new school before Aunt Suzanne left for Gabon because I wanted her to tell my father how I was doing in deep detail. So, the next day, I phoned Jean Noel and asked if we could meet. He eventually agreed and suggested that I met with him in downtown Manhattan.

I had not visited that part of the city, but I assured him I could find it. I knew that I just had to catch the train going downtown and get off on 32nd Street, and from there, walk to the hotel and ask for help whenever I felt lost. This was one of the good aspects of New Yorkers. In fact, something true to the city of New York is that there always was a person to help you locate a place you were having a tough time finding. Not all New Yorkers knew New York City, but at least one person had been in that place you were looking for and would be able to show you the way to get there. So, it did not take too long for me to locate the Pennsylvania Hotel and meet Jean Noel over there. He was inside when I arrived there.

Pennsylvania Hotel is a huge and high building on the other side of Madison Square Garden, a place in the city of New York where people come from all the world over to take pictures and keep memorable souvenirs because of the history of that area and the beauty of its surroundings. Being in the lobby of the Pennsylvania

Hotel was like being in a train station. People were all over the room causing much human traffic, which made it difficult to locate Jean Noel. Some sat on their luggage because no more benches were available; others preferred to stand and wait; while some others queued by the front desk, where everybody wanted to make a reservation or check in for rooms available. I stood there for a moment, mesmerized by the movement in the room. Where could Jean Noel be in this room? I did not know what to do because I did not have a cell phone yet; otherwise, I could have just given him a call and figured out where he was. By the time, I desperately began to think about exiting the room, someone hit my shoulder, and when I turned, it was Jean Noel carrying a school backpack. We greeted one another, and he asked what I thought about the place. I told him I did not have enough words to describe, but quite frankly I was amazed by the traffic in that hotel. Then I asked where the school was, and Jean returned the question back to me, asking that I guess where the school might be. I told him I had no clue but really wanted to know. He laughed after that and told me the school was inside that very hotel. When he said that, I looked at him with a surprised expression on my face. What sort of school could be in such an environment? Jean looked back at me and showed me the way to an elevator we were going to take, and while heading there, he told me the building was not only a hotel, but also incorporated business offices and a school of language. He continued by explaining that from a business perspective, it was efficient and well thought to have a school of language in such a busy hotel because most people who lived in the hotel were foreigners who came to New York for business or personal activities, and others even came as students from incredibly good families. They would rather have a school close to their living place than to have to go through New York City's traffic to get to a school in one of the many corners of the city. It sounded logical to me as well, and especially from the business perspective, I thought he was right.

When we reached the second floor, the door opened and we arrived in a room with a front desk representative. She was a beautiful young lady with a black-suited uniform that gave her a very professional appearance. She welcomed us and laughed at Jean. Because she recognized him, her attention turned to me. She nevertheless asked Jean if we were together. He told her I was his brother and that I needed to transfer to the school for the next session. The lady smiled at me, and while pulling a pile of copies out of a drawer, she asked how long I had been in New York City. I smiled back, trying to be a gentleman, and told her I had been there for a month. "You just got out of the boat, man!" That is what she said, and even though I did not get what she meant at that moment, I smiled and told her I was brand new in the city. The papers she handed over to me were some sort of application that she asked I fill out before she sent me to an advisor. She gave me a pen as well, and while standing there, I began to fill out the documents with information about my past education and some personal information as well. When I finished with those documents, she asked me to have a seat on one the chairs on the other side of her desk. Jean told me he needed to go back to class because he was not done yet, but he would like that I wait for him after I was done with the advisor. I agreed and he left while I got myself a chair. I was not the only one to sit there. It looked just like an interview room where people went to be asked questions about their employment history and their life and so forth. There were some other people waiting for an advisor to receive them, and the funny thing about it was that there were about four different languages being spoken around me. One group spoke Spanish, another spoke Arabic, another French, and another a language I did not know at all and had never heard before. I felt very attracted by the latter, and after a moment of trying to figure out what language it was, I decided to ask them what they spoke. One gentleman kindly responded and told me he was from India and he spoke a dialect that I do not recall the name of anymore. I knew it was a pretty weird language, but it was fascinating to listen to. The man asked where I was from, and I told him I was from Africa and more precisely Gabon. He said he had never heard about it before. I told him I understood that was probably because my country was a small one among the many well-known countries of Africa. He asked what language I spoke, and I told him French, but added that I did have a dialect as well and that certainly he would not know anything about it. He laughed after I said that and asked if I could tell him "Hello" in my dialect. I smiled at him and said "MBOLO." He tried to say it, but with his accent and the hard contraction of the language, it sounded more like "MBOALO." I laughed so loudly the young lady came over and asked if everything was all right. I excused myself and told her everything was okay. She returned to her desk and the guy from India looked at me and sent me another smile, which I responded to with my own. We made it funny in the room. He told me his name, but due to its complexity, I cannot recall it today. He asked if I knew who my advisor was, and I told him I did not, but surely was going to find out soon. After I said that, the lady at the front desk called my name and asked that I walk out to the aisle and there should be an office on my left, where I would meet with Mr. Octavio. That was the name of the man who was going to be my advisor, and when I reached his office, he surprised me by saying my last name as correctly as a Gabonese would say it. He called me "Mr. Ebang." Nobody had called me that since my arrival in the States, especially a non-African who said it with the correct accent. I asked him how that was possible. He told me he received students from many parts of the world every day and certainly that explained him saying my name correctly. I told him I felt particularly good to hear it and I would love for him to call me that. He agreed to do so, and while pulling another pile of documents from his drawer, he asked where I was from. Just like I responded to my friend from India, I told him I was from Africa and more precisely, a country called Gabon. He did not seem surprised to hear that, and before I even added anything, he told me he had had many students from Gabon in the past years and even believed many still were attending the school. I said to myself, "Well, Frank, that's an international school you are getting into." The man gave me a pile of documents, which he required I take with me to read information about the school and how I would like to organize my class schedule. I thanked him and left the office. By the time, I was done with Mr. Octavio, my friend Jean Noel also was done with his class, so I met him by the elevator entry and we both got in and exited Pennsylvania Hotel. Jean asked if I liked the place and if I would love to be there. I told him it was exactly what I was looking for. One thing that I liked about the school was that it gave you a choice of what your class schedule was going to be, if you stayed within the hours required for foreign students. At the other school, I could not make a schedule of my own, and I just thought that was a plus for me, especially since I was thinking about getting a part-time job sometime soon. Jean told me he had been attending that school for a year and was almost done. I showed him the folder with the document Mr. Octavio gave me. Jean smiled after I handed the folder over to him, and I asked what was funny about it. He, then, explained to me that he was too received the same folder after he registered for courses at ALCC, but he never actually had a look at them because he thought it was too much reading and he did not have time for that. Well, I understood that Jean was not a fan of reading that day, and I told him that I enjoyed reading and could spend an entire day at the library just looking at books and having an enjoyable time there. We laughed at each other about that while heading toward a subway station to catch an uptown train. I was happy with myself that day and when I got home, I told Aunt Suzanne about the school whose name was ALCC, which stood for American Language Communication Center. Aunt Suzanne told me she knew about that school but was thinking about another school named ZONI, which she thought would be interesting as well. I asked if she had information about that school and how much it cost to attend. She handed a booklet about that school to me and told me to compare it to ALCC so I could choose the one I felt more comfortable with. I told her I would do so later that night after I read about both schools. Aunt Suzanne did not stay up too late anymore, as she spent most of her days purchasing things that she was going to take with her back home, and when she arrived at the apartment, she needed to pack them and make sure her luggage was ready for the day she was scheduled to leave. So, she would fall asleep as soon as she closed her luggage.

The next day, I had to call Ms. Rebecca and tell her I was not going to attend the other session at ESL but at ALCC, and therefore, I would need them to transfer my records to Mr. Octavio, my new advisor at ALCC. She told me she would just need a letter from ALCC, saying that I was enrolling at their establishment. So, I called Jean and asked if he were going to be at school that day, but he let me know that he was not going to have class that day so I would have to go meet with my advisor by myself. I thanked Jean and told him I would head to Pennsylvania Hotel. I promised to let him know how things turned out. Before I headed to ALCC, I made sure I took all my documents with me to make things easier for the advisor. Mr. Octavio had a very cool humor, and when he saw me walking by his office, he called my name just the way he did the day we first met. I liked that from him. He asked if I had read the documents he handed me the other day, and I told him I did look at them and decided to enroll with ALCC. He filled out some other parts of the documents and told me I was all set for to begin next session as soon as I was ready and could decide what my schedule was going to be. He added that we did not have to talk about the financial part of the registration until I chose my schedule and my classes. Everything sounded good to me and I hurried to get back home and call my father, hoping that he had resolved the scholarship issue and I could be expecting to have it before the beginning of my session. Unfortunately, I heard the most devastating news I could expect to hear as far as my education was concerned. My father in fact did go to the office in charge of granting scholarships, and they let him know that I was not going to receive that scholarship for some reason that they could not even tell him. My father was a man of exceptional temper and before such a reality, he did not want to argue with them and ask for their true motive for freezing my scholarship. "What are we going to do now?" I asked my father. Calmly with his habitual voice, he told me to keep my mind cool because he believed in a God that would never let him down and because of that, everything was going to be all right. I did not want to add anything after my father said so because I, too believed that there was a God who had a plan for everyone's life and if we took our burdens and handed them to him, he would find a way to reduce their weight on us. But still, I kept thinking about how hard this was going to be on my father and the whole family. This was the beginning of what was going to be a long race for me in the land of giants – a land that I did not yet know the true realities of and to what extent things could really get too. Realizing that I was not going to have a scholarship, I began to have a different picture of where I was. Everything was suddenly darkening for me, and the sweet-sugar taste of life in New York that I had been enjoying was beginning to turn into a bitter taste completely unknown to me. Why such an injustice? I mean, I did study hard in high school to deserve my scholarship just like anybody else who had done so. What could lead to this decision? I was among the best students of my graduation class, if not the best, and now, I was going to have to pay for my education, a price I knew was not going to be easy at all on my parents.

After spending, a few hours meditating and questioning my destiny in the USA, I decided to just let things and see what happened. When Aunt Suzanne got home, I told her about the news and she just looked at me sadly. I could see the expression in her eyes when she told me that it was because of things like this that she could not stay in Gabon and teach there, anymore. In fact, she knew about my academic successes, as she once was my teacher. Aunt Suzanne told me not to worry because I was not the only student from Gabon who was in such a situation in the USA. In fact, she added that she knew many more students who experienced that exact situation and the whole story lay in some political matters that we students could not understand. After she mentioned the political side of these sorts of injustices, I began to think that because my father excluded himself from the political games of the country, even though many government people asked him to engage in them, I was being somehow targeted to make him change his mind. I told Aunt Suzanne about the school and all that I discussed with Mr. Octavio. She told me that she needed to go with me to ALCC and meet my advisor so we could discuss the financial side of the process before she left for Gabon. I agreed with her and we decided that we were going to make it there the following day. I was beginning to learn that sometimes things in life did not always go the way we expected them to go, but that should never be a reason to give up and let go of everything. This was a moment for me to strengthen my determination and desire to achieve my goals and reach the peak of the mountain. It was just the beginning of the climbing, and the denial of my scholarship was just the beginning of the race for me. I said my prayer that night and asked that God be with me throughout that process and to give me the power to always stand up and never stay down.

At around ten the following morning, Aunt Suzanne and I headed to see Mr. Octavio. I asked Aunt Suzanne if she knew the Pennsylvania Hotel. She laughed loudly and asked me what I was thinking. She knew the Pennsylvania Hotel and had already heard about ALCC but had never been to the school's location. I told her I was impressed the first time I went with Jean Noel and never could I imagine that there was a school in a hotel. New York City was such an amazing place. I had been living there for almost two months and still everything looked brand new to me. We arrived at ALCC and asked the front desk lady if Mr. Octavio was available, as we had not called in advance to arrange an appointment with him. The lady asked that we wait while she went to check on him. She came back after a few minutes and asked that we follow her to Mr. Octavio's desk.

"Hello, Mr. Ebang!" He greeted me and I responded while introducing Aunt Suzanne to him. I told him that we came to discuss the financial requirements and that I was ready to make my schedule with him. He pulled out my folder from one drawer and handed a class schedule to me. I had the choice between evening classes and morning classes. I asked Aunt Suzanne what she thought I should do. She told me it would be good for me to take evening classes so that I could look for a job in the mornings. She added that this was the way many other students were doing it there. I then told Mr. Octavio that I was going to take evening classes. He entered that information in his computer and gave me some other documents to sign to certify that I had the choice of time for my classes. After we dealt with the class schedule, he handed another document to me and explained that I needed to have my financial sponsor fill it out and bring a bank statement with the amount of $3,000 as a present balance in it. That document was necessary for him to issue a new I-20 to me, as I needed a new one to maintain my Visa status. He added that because classes were starting next week, I needed to have all these documents ready as soon as possible; otherwise, I could not even register for the session and this could jeopardize my immigration status. Aunt Suzanne thanked the man and told him we were going to have the documents ready in the next two days and come back for registration. We left the office and, on our way, back, I did not say anything because I did not know what to say and how we were going to have $3,000 in the next two days. My father was certainly going to provide the money for me to pay for classes, but I was not too sure he could find $3,000 in the next two days from his bank statement. I felt awfully bad inside, and it seemed as if the whole world was falling over my head. I left home with a heart filled with determination and hope that things were going to be all right and that I just needed to believe they would. But now was another lesson that I was learning. It took more than believing that things were going to be all right. It took more than being optimistic and waiting for things to change to our advantage. What I truly needed to understand was that life was not easy at all, and with determination must come the affirmative action that pushed me to tackle the difficulties and obstacles with a never-let-go mind. There was going to be a solution for the problem before me, and I just needed to pull myself together and seek for means to solve the issue. I looked at Aunt Suzanne and she did not even seem bothered. Then I understood that she had a plan and her attitude showed her maturity in dealing with situations like these. I needed to become mature enough to control my emotions. In fact, I began to realize that I had spent most of my time trying to grow my intellect while not allowing time for the growth of my personality. Did I even have a personality? What could I really say about myself that did not relate to my academic report? I needed to create a picture of who I really was and how I could be defined as a man in society. I surely could talk about my father's personality and his principles of life, but what about mine? Did I even have any principles of life? Again, I thought my race in the land of giants was not going to be an easy one, nor a short one. Sometimes we thought and even believed that we knew what the priority for us really was, but life had a way of proving us wrong, and when that happened, we were tempted to give up instead of backing up a little bit and staring the race over.

Coming to America, for me was the greatest opportunity offered to reach all my academic goals. I first thought I was going to live in a dormitory or something like that. I had the image of those big universities I used to see in movies about college life in the U.S. My sole and only job was going to be reading and passing tests or exams. I did not think that I was going to have to wake up the sleeping man inside of me. I did not even believe that I would need to find a job to provide for some of my basic needs and help my parents pay for my education. My whole hope laid on my scholarship, which I knew could exempt me from some financial hardship. Now, it was time to wake up and look at life with a different eye. It was time for me to take things the way they came to me and not drop my dreams.

Later that same day, as we got home, I asked Aunt Suzanne what she thought we should do. She asked me if I thought that my father could have the $3,000 in his account in the next two days. I told her that I did not believe he could, as I knew that he was going to ask for a bank loan to pay for my first session at ALCC. She told me she was going to see some of her friends and have them lend her some money so she could deposit it in her account and sign the document as my sponsor and after everything was done, she would return the money to her friends. I did not think about something like that and could not even imagine that could be possible. But Aunt Suzanne assured me not to worry at all and that she was going to meet with one good friend of hers whom she would introduce to me because I needed to personally meet her and express my gratitude if she made it possible. I thought it was a great idea and could not wait for the next day so we could meet the lady. I now was experiencing the truth in my father's words, when he told me that God never forgets his children and will always find a way out of no way. I felt a lot better after hearing Aunt Suzanne's idea. I felt relieved from a long pain, and even if we did not have a positive answer yet from her friend, I still liked the situation better. At the same time, I decided to thank God for allowing Aunt Suzanne to be with me during that moment of turbulence. I did not know what I would have done, had I been alone. It was becoming clear to me that God did not do anything just for the sake of doing it, and therefore everything eventually came with a purpose. I needed then to understand that even those hardships came with a purpose, and the very fact that I was not going to have a scholarship to pay for my education in America did have a purpose, which I needed to figure out and accept.

Tete was the lady's name; at least that's how Aunt Suzanne called her. She had been living in the States, and in New York City for years now. We met with her somewhere in downtown Manhattan; I just cannot remember where exactly, because I had not been there before. But I could see that there was a public sitting place where I noticed some guys were getting their hair braided while others played checkers and many other types of get-together activities. Aunt Suzanne introduced me to the lady, and while doing so, she told the lady I was her nephew and the one she had talked to her about. Tate looked at me with a nice, smiling face. "Oh! Nice to meet you, Frank. Your aunt told me about your problem, and I am surely going to help you with that." I slowly but deeply thanked the lady as we kept walking along the street and she engaged in other conversation with Aunt Suzanne. I felt lucky that I could now begin to really enjoy the atmosphere and all the goings-on of downtown Manhattan. People were from various parts of the world; I could tell by the many languages I heard while walking among people. It was amazing how all those people could get together in one country and feel free to speak their dialects with no limitations or restrictions from anybody. I wanted to speak my own dialect with Aunt Suzanne, just to see what it would feel like. But I restrained myself from speaking because Tete would not understand anything, as she belonged to a different ethnic group and therefore, it would not be appropriate and nice to do so, especially after she had agreed to do me such an important favor. As we kept walking, Tete asked if I already had a bank account. I told her yes and added that I was banking with City Bank. She said that it was even better because she also banked with City Bank, and therefore, it would make the transaction more efficient and faster so I could just print out my bank statement and present it to Mr. Octavio for him to complete my file and deliver my new I-20. After walking along the street for a while, Aunt Suzanne and Tete proposed that we look for a place where we could eat lunch. Tete suggested that we go for a Chinese buffet so we could have diversity in our choice of what we wanted to eat. Aunt Suzanne thought the idea was good and I could not say otherwise since I had not been to a buffet before and could not wait to see what it was like to eat there. I first thought it was going to be Chinese food, since Tete said a Chinese buffet, but later when we got there, I was surprised by the variety of food in there. Aunt Suzanne explained to me that in a buffet, we just needed to pay once and would have access to everything on the menu if we wanted to stay there. This was amazing to me, and I could only think of the many times I wanted to sit in a restaurant for hours, going from one order to the other. The room was almost filled up, and I could understand the reason for it to be like that. I mean, it was about five dollars, and people would come from various places just to eat there. One lady after each of us had a plate filled with our different choices and told us we could go upstairs because they still had open seating there. This was even better for me, because from where she led us, you had a beautiful view of outside and could contemplate the beauty of Manhattan while enjoying a delicious meal. I certainly was having a wonderful day with Aunt Suzanne and Tete, and I wished deeply inside of me that every day be just like that – free of sorrows, negative thoughts, worries, and everything else that could disturb your mind. We sat in the Chinese buffet for about an hour as I kept trying different meals, and Aunt Suzanne and Tete kept talking about things I did not have a clue about. Then, we left and Tete gave me her phone number so I could call her anytime I needed to when Aunt Suzanne left for Gabon. She said I should not hesitate to call her, and that by the next day, she would make the transaction for me so everything would work fine. I gave her a hug and thanked her again for everything. Aunt Suzanne told her she was going to call her when she arrived in Libreville because she was leaving soon. Tete wished her a safe trip and recommended her in the hands of God during her whole stay back home. We separated, and Aunt Suzanne and I began looking for an uptown train station where we could catch the Line 1 heading to Harlem. Because we were far from train stations, we decided to walk a little bit and reach downtown, not too far from 42nd street.

We walked there, and as we kept going, Aunt Suzanne told me that she was leaving tomorrow morning and needed to make sure that everything was going to be fine for me. I told her how thankful I was and how she could count on me to take care of the apartment until she returned. She told me she had arranged for me to have a roommate, and the guy was going to meet with us later that evening so we could meet each other and he could see the room before she left. I was a little surprised with that news, but I soon realized that it was actually a clever idea, as we were going to share the rent and this would allow me to save more of whatever funds I had with me. I got into the train, and while looking for a free seat, I asked Aunt Suzanne how she had met Tete. She told me they met during some church activities. I knew that Aunt Suzanne was regularly active in church activities and did commit to religious growth. Many times, I had seen her leave the room for church meetings at night where they would have praying activities, religious concerts, and so many other activities she participated in with her church, which was called The Great Refuge Temple. I remember one Sunday; she asked that I go with her so I could appreciate the way her church worshiped the Lord. The Great Refuge Temple, I would say, was an all-Black Pentecostal church located in the very center of Harlem, on the left side of the street across from Adam Clayton Powel Blvd and 125th Street. The church was founded in 1966 by the senior pastor, Bishop W.L. Bonner. It was in one giant building, neighboring several stores. Looking at the building from the outside did not really tell of what was on the inside. When we approached the building on that Sunday, I thought it was some small, but certainly nice-looking church in Harlem. I was not appreciating what that church truly was. By the time, we got into the building, I could not help holding my mouth to express my astonishment before the high standard and quality of the church. It appeared just as one of those huge rooms I used to see on TV, where very well-known and professional opera personalities went to perform. The room was not only large in the availability of its space, but it also stood high, with seats surrounding the whole room. How was this possible? I asked myself, especially for a Black church in Harlem. I had underestimated the value of that church at first sight. I was now receiving my first sermon of the day. I had expected the church to be some small congregation, not unlike the many other churches in the Harlem area, at least from some of those that I had visited before. I learned that I should not judge anything by how it looked from the outside. It was the inside that determined every being, and if we spent more time trying to look at the inside and understand it in everybody we met, then the world certainly would be a better place to live in. The Great Refuge Temple was just as the name said it was, "great." Aunt Suzanne smiled at my funny facial expression and proudly told me, "That's my church and I love it." Everybody in the room was dressed up just the way someone would dress if they had to meet the President of the United States. There was in the room every category of individual: children, adolescents, adults, very aged individuals – but all of them had in common their very elegant style of dress; that mesmerized me. I realized at that moment the value those people gave to Sunday in their church and what it really meant for them.

Everybody greeted everybody, some laughing from one side to the other, others on their knees and in prayer, while others sang praises to the Lord. I mean, the whole room was alive and I could feel the very touch of the spirit all over my body. It felt good and I had not even heard the sermon. I was now sure I could say to myself: This place is holy. Aunt Suzanne told me we needed to go upstairs and get a seat up there so we could have a broad view of the room and the auditorium. We walked up the stairs, and by the time we got there and I looked down and around me, the view was absolutely amazing. I did not know what to say anymore and I just headed toward a seat I thought would be fine for me, as it really gave me a pleasant view of the front and the entire room as well. Aunt Suzanne picked a seat close to mine so we could talk to each other whenever we wanted to do so. The service began after an hour of people individually worshiping and praising the glory of the Lord. I did enjoy sitting there and observing everyone else in their worshiping. I almost forgot that I was to be worshiping my Lord; instead, I felt like I was in a movie theatre, waiting for the movie to start. I did not even notice that next to me, Aunt Suzanne was already in deep worship, praying and chanting how wonderful God had been to her and her entire family. She was possessed by a strong spiritual force; I guess I should say that she was filled with the Holy Ghost, and her voice began to sound different from the one I was familiar with. At this moment, I felt an urgency to get into myself and begin to think about what the Lord had done for me, and how I could be thankful for Him. The experience was overwhelming, and I could not stop thinking about how I felt in total harmony with the whole church and with myself. I realized at that moment the truth in that scripture in which Jesus said to his disciples that wherever two or three people would gather in his name, He would be among them. The Great Refuge Temple was a holy place and one did not have to be spiritually engaged in a personal relationship with God to feel it while attending a service there. The sermon on that Sunday was delivered by the church founder, Bishop Lee Boner, and before he stepped before the pulpit to deliver his message, the church's major choir heated up the entire room and the attendants, with a vibrant selection of gospel songs from "Happy Day" to "Glory is Thy Faithfulness," which I believed were famous gospel songs mostly from the old Negro spirituals. I felt vivified and pushed to opening my eyes and envisioning the very foundation of the history of Black people in America and what the church really represented for these descendants of African slaves.

For a moment, everything seemed so personal to me that even the message delivered by Bishop Lee Bonner seemed one arranged just for me. He talked about each of us being sent to Earth with a personal mission from the Lord and that we should never stop struggling until we achieved that mission. He added that God never abandoned his children, and that because of his love for us, he would always sustain us in moments of troubles or hardships of any sort. The message was a strong one, and I remembered that after the service, I asked Aunt Suzanne if I could go meet with the man and tell him how deeply his sermon touched me. She said we certainly could manage to meet him, but because of the traffic on the way out and the flow of people who also rushed to meet with Bishop Lee Bonner, we decided to let it go and hope to do so some other time. It was in that church that Aunt Suzanne and Tete met. One could easily understand the strong bound that existed between the two, as it was a spiritual bond, one that was settled in the name of the Lord Jesus Christ.

I also recall one lady that Aunt Suzanne introduced me to. I do not know what her name really was, but I recalled that everyone, including Aunt Suzanne, called her sister Ig, so I would call her sister Ig. She was a highly active member of the Great Refuge Temple and was also involved in the evangelization of those who had not accepted the Lord yet and wished to do so. Sister Ig was a very tall and elegant woman. She was originally from Hawaii and had moved to New York City for personal reasons I did not know, but she joined the church and took it as a call from the Lord to serve him and spread his word to those who had not yet experienced a life with Christ. Sister Ig was one of the first persons to encourage me to author a book about my life. Somehow, after the service and while the crowd was beginning to walk away from the church's building, we engaged into a conversation about how I came to be in the States and what my ambitions were and all that. Sister Ig stared at me the whole time I was telling her my story from my high school activities to my decision to come to America, get an education, and be an important personality in the development of not only my country, but the world. I spoke to Sister Ig about my dreams with passion, and I guess she could tell a lot about me at that moment. Before we said good-bye to each other, as Aunt Suzanne was about ready to leave, Sister Ig told me that I should author a book about my story from Gabon to America and everything else that would come during the pursuit of my destiny. I did not really feel the profoundness of Sister Ig's message, but I did say to her, while leaving with Aunt Suzanne, that I would think about it someday.

Aunt Suzanne was not ready to go to bed that night, and she kept loading stuff in her bags and asking me if I thought she was going to have to pay extra money for overweight bags. I told her she needed to balance her luggage and separate everything that weighed too much so she should carry things with her and let others go through bag checking. I could not sleep either, so we spent a good part of the night talking about how long she was going to stay back home and what she was going to say to my parents and my friends from high school about me. I also felt a little sad that night, even though I really felt like I needed to be just on my own and assess my sense of responsibility toward myself. At about seven o'clock the next day, Aunt Suzanne and I got up and began moving her luggage from the corner where they stood to the front door so we could easily grab them by the time we got a taxi to take her to JFK. But we also needed to be ready to meet with the guy who was going to share the room with me since Aunt Suzanne arranged to meet with him early that morning before she left. After about two hours, and we were all ready and waiting to call a cab, someone rang the bell downstairs and I pushed the button back to open the door for him.

"Certainly, it is Chris and he is a little late, though!" said Aunt Suzanne.

I walked toward the door to open it for him, as I heard him getting closer to our door.

"Hello! I am Chris! I suppose you are Frank?"

"Hi! Chris, I am in fact Frank, and it is good to meet you, man!"

I let Chris into the room and Aunt Suzanne welcomed him with that nice-looking facial expression of hers.

"Well, Chris, this is the place, and I was almost beginning to wonder if you were still going to come," Aunt Suzanne said.

"Yea! I am sorry, though. I was having problems trying to catch up the uptown train to get here, but here I am, and the place is okay for me."

Aunt Suzanne took her time to explain to Chris what she expected from us staying together, and she insisted that we needed to respect one another as two adults and if there was going to be any problem, we should give her a call so she could help us fix the issue. Chris seemed like a very cool guy to me and quite frankly, I did not find any reason we would not get along and have an enjoyable time as roommates. He was an exchange student at Brooklyn College from a partnership with his France-base university. I could not remember the name of his university in France, but he had been taking classes at Brooklyn College for a semester by that time. After we introduced each other, Aunt Suzanne suggested that we go downstairs with her luggage and look for a cab. It did take us long to walk down the stairs and get a cab for Aunt Suzanne, before helping her put her luggage in the vehicle's trunk.

She gave me a deep hug and told me to behave and take care of the place. She also gave Chris a hug and wished us good luck. While staring at the cab driving away from the building, I looked up into the sky and asked God to be with Aunt Suzanne during her trip and sojourn back home.

Chris and I went back in the room and tried to get to know each other more. Chris was originally from Rwanda but had lived in France since an early age with his sister. He majored in physics and chemistry, though I never was too interested in science, I respected that Chris really enjoyed what he studied, and he was good at those subjects. He also practiced martial arts and was Black Belt in Karate, "just the right guy to hang out with," I said to myself. I told Chris about my ambitions, and even though I had not achieved much yet, I wanted to Chris to know that I was serious about my studies too. He did not stay any longer after we talked a little more because he needed to pack all his things from where he stayed so he could be back before the day was over. I told him I was going to be absent for a while, as I wanted to go spend time with Jean Noel and Emile. I needed to do something to not feel the emptiness in the room with Aunt Suzanne having left. Chris told me he had a double of the key and therefore he should be fine whenever he brought his stuff. He left and I, too headed to the train station on 125th street, and meet with Jean and Emile afterwards.

It was windy outside, and it was about the time people rushed from every corner to get into a train station and head to their different directions, some running late to reach their working shifts, some high school students getting off for classes, while others made their way to school and so on and so forth. That is what it was like in most places in New York City, and I admitted that I had gotten myself used to that ambiance. When I reached Jean Noel's apartment, he was not there and so I decided to go upstairs to Emile's and maybe I could find him there as he made me understand that most of the time when he was not in his room, he certainly would be in Emile's and therefore I needed to go up there and check on him. In fact, by the time I reached Emile's room, Jean Noel was ready to leave from there; we met right when he was exiting Emile's room.

"Hey, Jean! I just checked in your room and I figured that you certainly must be upstairs."

"Hello, Frank! I was also leaving Emile's room. Since I had nothing to do in my room, I got bored. Has Aunt Suzanne left yet?"

"Yea, she left this morning and that's particularly the reason I decided to come stay with you guys for a while, since I sort of felt lonely."

Jean smiled a little bit when I mentioned that I did not want to feel lonely. He even joked that I should find myself a nice girl to keep me company while Aunt Suzanne was gone. We laughed on after that and both went back in Emile's room. I did not know how to better express it, but every time I got into Emile's room, I felt just as if I was somewhere in Libreville, visiting an old friend of mine. The atmosphere at Emile's place was one to fly you back home and remind you of the good times with your friends and family. The music was always by a Gabonese artist, like Pierre Claver Akendengue, Oliver Ngoma, Patience Dabany, or Landry Ifouta. I would automatically forget all my sad thoughts and get into a happy humor of rejoicing, and with a vigorous voice, I would say hello to Emile and ask him what he had to offer as a tough drink. He would begin to laugh at that before directing me to the refrigerator and leaving me to make my choice of drink. There would be Bud Light, Coors Light, Heineken, and other drinks I had never tasted before.

We sat there with Jean for about two hours, talking about everything and anything, just having a fun time. Then I was ready to leave, since I knew that Chris would be home and I needed to meet with him and help him move his stuff into the room. I excused myself to the guys and told them why I needed to go. Jean reminded me that we were to meet at school the next day. I felt that it would take me longer to get home if I walked to the train station. So, I decided to get a taxi and head straight home. That was easy to do, especially in that part of the neighborhood. When I got home, Chris was already in there, unpacking his things from his bags.

"Hey, Chris! How is it going? I am sorry, I had to go meet a few friends."

"You are fine, Frank. I just got here, too, and I was wondering what we were going to do with the closet so I could fit my clothes in there, too."

"There is no problem about it, Chris. I am going to just move mine and you would be able to fit yours too."

"Good, and thank you, Frank."

I was excited to have a roommate, and Chris again seemed like a very cool guy. We spent good hours of that night trying to make room for him to arrange his clothes and all his school stuff. Also, we got to know each other better, talking about what we liked to do and what we did not like at all. Chris told me he really enjoyed New York City and did not think about returning to France at all after his program was over. He explained that he did not know why he would have to go back to France when he could attend the best schools in the world here in the States. I thought he was right about that and I even encouraged him to think about a transfer after his program was over. We both laughed about the comparisons we tried to make between life in France and life in New York City. I told him I had never been to France, but I knew relatives who had been living there for a long time. He really knew about France; he grew up there and so he could talk to me about things I had no clue about. What was interesting was his French accent; Chris really spoke French just as if he were born and raised there. I found it interesting and funny at the same time, because, despite his very French accent, he seemed not to like it at all, and everything that he said about France was of no match with how he felt about life in New York City after only a year of residency. We ended up going to sleep late that night, but really, we had an enjoyable time that night.

The next day, I was the first to get up and get to the shower, as I knew how it worked in the building if you wanted to take your time in the shower. When I woke Chris up and reminded him that he had class, as he told me to do so if I woke up first, he jumped from his bed and for a minute looked at me like someone who had just seen an alien or something.

"What time is it, Frank?"

I told him it was about eight o'clock and I was heading to school. He quickly got up from where he sat, grabbed his towel, and exited the room in direction of the bathroom. It did not take ten seconds, and Chris was back to the room looking crazy. I asked him what was wrong, and he told me the door was locked. I calmly walked out so I could see why the door was locked. When I got closer, I noticed that there was someone in the shower. I looked at Chris and told him there was someone in the room. He looked with a lost expression on his face; I realized that he was still sleeping and none of what I am saying was making sense to him.

"Come on, Chris, you need to wake up! There is someone in the bathroom and you have to wait for that person to leave the room," I said.

Clearly Chris was not fully awake, he forced his eyes open and looked at me all confused.

"Oh! I am sorry, Frank. I was still sleeping and that happens to me all the time and I do not even realize what is going on."

I told him he was okay and that he would need to work on that and get up early if he wanted to use the bathroom without having to hurry because the neighbors also shared the same bathroom. I wished him a wonderful day and left the room since I needed to stop by the bank to get my bank statement, as I needed to bring it to Mr. Octavio to complete my proof of financial support. I knew that Tete had already deposited the money in my account so I should be able to effectively fulfill all the requirements and be able to attend my first class that morning. Mr. Octavio was also expecting me that day, so when I arrived at ALCC, the lady at the front desk, with her usual smile, greeted me and directed me to Mr. Octavio's desk.

"Good morning, Sir Ebang! How are we doing today?"

"Good morning, Mr. Octavio. I am doing great and ready to start class, as I have with me the rest of the documents you needed to establish a new I-20 for me."

"Well, sure, Mr. Ebang, I believe you should be able to go to class after this."

I presented the bank statement to him and he looked at it for a minute, then made a copy of it and put it in my folder. After that, he grabbed a document that looked like a class schedule.

"Here is your class schedule, Mr. Ebang, and you can see the name of your instructors and your different classrooms. I hope you have a fun time at ALCC and come to me anytime you have a problem."

I thanked Mr. Octavio and left his desk with a big smile betraying my excitement and the feeling of relief that filled my mind after that. I did not have to attend any class until six p.m. because I told Mr. Octavio that I would like to attend evening classes so I could have the mornings free to look for a job. Mr. Octavio, as well as most advisors at ALCC, was very understanding about that issue. They knew what it was like living in New York City and the necessity of having a job and being able to pay the bills. However, I still wanted to meet with Jean that morning, so I decided to stay there and wait for him to get out for a break so at least I could let him know my schedule and how things worked out.

ALCC had a nice student environment. The diversity of students made the uniqueness of that institution. The world over attended ALCC, a true United Nations establishment, I would say. Not only was the cost of classes affordable for all, but I could feel the positive atmosphere in the school through the faculty members, the advisors, and just everyone from the few times I had been there to complete my registration process. I knew that I would love to study there the first time I went in. After I waited for about thirty minutes, I saw

Jean walking out of a classroom. I waved at him to let him know I had waited for him. He walked over and asked how I did. I told him I made it fine and that was going to attend evening classes only. Jean felt a little lost when I told him I was going to attend evening classes, but he soon understood when I told him that I needed to look for a job in the morning so I could help pay the rent and take care of myself in general.

"I would have wanted you to take morning classes so we could at least talk every day, and why not get some of the fine girls you certainly met in here."

"I know, Jean. Me, too, but I really need to find a job, man."

"Yea, I got you on that, Frank, and even though I have a scholarship and it pays for my school, I still feel the need to have a job and keep up with life in here, man. It is not easy at all."

I did not know that Jean had a scholarship until that moment. We never actually talked about it before, but when he told me that he had a scholarship and that was how his studies were paid, I felt somehow hurt within. It brought back the thought of what it would have been like for me if my scholarship had not been taken away. But I decided not to bring the subject up at that moment even though it was unfair for me. Jean was not responsible for what happened to my scholarship. He was just lucky that his was being paid to him. I told him we could still meet, though, especially on weekends or whenever I did not have class and wanted to hang out. Because he had to go back to class, we said good-bye to each other, and I left the school building. The next step for me was to call Tete and let her know that how things went with Octavio and that I was ready to give her money back. Since I did not have a cell phone yet, I had to go back home and use the home phone. I called Tete once I got there, and she told me we could meet at Emile's sometime over the weekend since she did not have any free time to meet with me during the week. I thanked her and we finally scheduled to meet the coming Saturday at Emile's place.

The fact that Tete knew Emile surprised me, since she was more of a religious woman of the type who would not hang out with those who did not share her beliefs. But here she was asking that we meet at Emile's place, where I knew only of the drinking, loud talking, and all noise happening. Well, it just told me how good of a guy Emile really was to his people and everybody who knew him. I thought for the rest of my day, I would go look for a job, and the best way to do so was to just get on the streets of New York City and walk from one corner to the other, stopping in different stores, restaurants, and any place where business activity was possible. One important thing to point out while going along with my story is that it never took me too long to get a job. Even though I was not always hired, I stopped at few places to fill out applications. While most guys in my situation would struggle to find a job, I got offers without too much effort. Most young Africans, or foreigners I saw in the city were doing jobs like dishwasher, servers, bartender, or they were simply selling newspapers inside and outside train-stations. I walked in Harlem from every side, looking for a job but no one was hiring. As I continued to look for a job, I wondered about the whole situation and how it was going to affect my life, my studies, the very reason I came to America for. Now, I was looking for a job so I could be able to take care of myself and somehow help my father by reducing the load of his expenses to take care of my stay in America. Often, I saw other young people just like me, looking for jobs, and when I stopped to share words with them, stories were close to the same. It was either they needed to find a job to send to their families back home to whatever country they came from, or to pay a bill, sometimes, just like me, they needed to save money to pay for school.

After about a week, looking for a job while going to ALCC late in the evenings, I received a call from a lady named Ruth. She was the owner and manager of a small coffee shop and restaurant that I stopped at in Riverdale, New York, exactly on the other side of the Bronx. It took me about forty-five minutes to get there. She was ready to hire me as a dishwasher and also make deliveries to customers who ordered from the restaurant. When I arrived at Nonis Restaurant, I first noticed how busy that place was. People entered and left every ten minutes. I imagined, the load of work in that place, and while I was excited about the opportunity, I wondered if I was going to be able to keep up.

Ruth met me at the door and asked if I was Frank. I told her I was, and she asked that I follow her to the back of the restaurant so we could talk about what she wanted me to do. When we got there, I was first surprised by how huge the place really was. In fact, from the entrance, one would assume that the place was simply built with a front room where guests would enjoy their breakfast or lunch and a small area where the cook and his guys would take care of all the kitchen stuff. This would not be accurate, though, because the back of the room was not that small of an area. It was a spacious room that led to a basement; one needed to go down about twenty stairs to get in there. There she called the stock room. Everything that was used to fix orders was safely stocked in the basement. There were three big freezers where she kept everything that needed to be in such a temperature: meat, fish, chicken, and a whole variety of what composed the menu at Nonis Restaurant. Ruth was Hispanic; I would say she was from the Dominican Republic since her Spanish accent sounded to me more like that of Hispanics, I heard speaking whenever I went to Emile's place, where a sizable number of Dominicans resided. She spoke English very well, though, with a Spanish accent that made it attractive. She was not very tall, but I barely could say that I was taller than she. One could guess Ruth's temper at first sight. She was a remarkably busy woman, always ready to pick up the phone and take orders; at the same time, she would go look in the kitchen to see how the cook was doing with the orders she sent. Then she would go in the back room to check on the dishes.

I stood there for a while, as she went about showing me the things I had to do when I arrived to work. She explained that she needed me to make sure the dishes were clean always, from when I got there to when I was ready to leave. I had to assure her that the front of the restaurant was clean because as we were entering winter, leaves would fall from the trees around the restaurant cover every side around. Also, I had to sweep and mop the front room before I could leave. When she was done explaining what she expected from me, Ruth looked at me with a profoundly serious expression before asking if I thought I could do the job. I told Ruth that I could do the job and was even ready to start that very day if she wanted me to. Deep inside of myself, I knew that this was not going to be easy for me, especially as I had never done anything like that before. I decided to go for it, as I did not really have a choice. Ruth laughed a little bit at the way I responded to her and she told me she believed that I could do it since I was from Africa. We both shared the joke and she asked me what language I spoke. I told Ruth that I was from Gabon and my official language was French, but I also knew Spanish and English. When I told her that I knew Spanish, she appeared incredibly surprised and asked in Spanish, "Como aprendiste Español?" so to know how I managed to learn Spanish. I replied in Spanish and told her that I learned Spanish in high school while in Gabon and that it was common for Gabonese to know Spanish since it was mandatory in classes. I knew that the fact that I spoke Spanish helped make my relationship with Ruth easier. She was glad that I spoke her language. She made it clear to me that I should not be surprised if sometimes she spoke to me only in Spanish. I told her it would be simply fine for me and would even be great for me to practice some more. Then she introduced me to the chief cook. His name was Pedro. He was from Mexico and had been working for Ruth for an exceptionally long time so they really got along well and would throw jokes at each other throughout the shift. When I told Pedro, I was Frank, and Ruth added that I spoke Spanish as well, he decided to call me Don Franco if I was okay with that. I agreed and told him it did not matter at all. I really was ready to start that very day, but Ruth suggested that I start the next day. I had to be there at seven o'clock to open with her and leave at three p.m. The schedule was simply perfect for me, as I did not start class until six p.m. I had time to go back home and get ready for class after work.

So, I left Nonis Restaurant that day and promised Ruth that I would be on time the next day to start my job. I was happy with that and on my way home, I thanked God for blessing me with the opportunity that came at a moment I was beginning to lose hope about getting a job. I heard my father's words in my mind when he said that I should never forget that his God would never abandon me. It was beginning to get very cold at that moment, as we were reaching the middle of November. My reaction to the winter was not good at all. I noticed that at moments, whenever it got very cold outside, I would have blood coming out of my nose and my ears would begin to hurt so badly that I would need to put a lotion on them every time I felt the pain. Most people I talked to about those reactions told me it was normal and that with time, I would begin to feel better as my body learned to adapt to the changing seasons and their effects on my body system. Sometimes, I wished I were enjoying the beautiful sun of Libreville, especially when we were getting off from school, waiting for a taxi or a school bus to pick us up. I had to get used to the cold, though, as I would get up every morning except Sunday to go to Riverdale at early hours of the day. There were days when I wanted to stay in bed because of the cold, but I reminded myself that Ruth and everybody at the restaurant counted on me, so I could not miss work.

I remembered those days when I had just arrived in New York City and when in a train, I noticed that most people slept without realizing so and would wake up and find out that they had missed their stop.

I once asked Aunt Suzanne what was wrong with those people. She did not say much about it if that certainly they lacked hours of sleep or just worked long hours. I was now in the exact same boat. I would find myself, on my way back home from Riverdale, sleeping in the train and sometimes realizing that I had passed my station. It was funny sometimes, but very annoying also. I worked at Nonis Restaurant for almost two months, and the longer I was there, the more I got comfortable with falling asleep in the train.

The experience at Nonis allowed me to build working skills I did not realize I had until I started working there. The first days were very rough, as I needed to get used to the language of the restaurant and the names of different condiments, as Pedro who stayed with me in the kitchen would send me down to the basement to look for a condiment, he needed to fix an order. It was a whole different education that I was receiving over there. I still remember when Ruth asked if I knew how to mop. I told her yes, I knew, but I did not know what she was talking about when she asked that I get the broom and the mop to clean a spot after a guest had left the place and had spilled his drink. I stood before her for a moment looking a little stupid and making her realize that I did not understand what she was talking about. It took for Pedro to get the bucket and the mop to show me what Ruth was asking me to do. The situation, although funny, made me feel uncomfortable, but I imagined that Ruth did not take it seriously, as she surely understood that I had no clue about what she was talking. Sometimes, she thought that it was a language issue. Soon, I became the man of the place. Pedro could easily ask that I bring condiments for him, and I would know where to get them and exactly what quantity he needed. Ruth would have me deliver some orders and it would not take me long to find the various locations and make my deliveries before going back to my dishes, making sure everything was clean and ready for use. We felt like a family at Nonis Restaurant – and Ruth, I began to look at her as more of a mother than as a boss. She would ask me to stop my dishes for a while and go sit with her in the front while she asked

Pedro to fix something for me to eat. One day, I remember the day was going slow, and she asked that I join her in the front. We began talking about my school and the things I wanted to do in my life. I told Ruth that I was going to go back one day to school and attend an Ivy league school to later work at the United Nations. She took me very seriously and told me that she believed I would make it and that I needed to remember her place whenever I got done with school and became somebody important. We laughed about it, but I promised Ruth that I would remember her place and that every time I would find myself in New York City, I would visit her. Pedro looked at me from the kitchen window and said something in Spanish that sounded like encouraging words, saying that I should also remember him. They were family for me now, and it could not be otherwise, as I spent my days at Nonis Restaurant before going to ALCC. There were days I longed to go to Nonis and skip classes at ALCC. I already had the level of English I needed to oversee conversations with anybody, and going to ALCC, although I would admit that classes were interesting, it felt more like fulfilling a formality. I had to be there to maintain my student status with the Immigration Department, which required that every international student have at least eighteen hours of classes per week. I could not do otherwise, and even if there were days that I could not make it to class on time because I fell asleep when I got home to change, I always managed to have my eighteen hours of classes by the end of the week.

My time became very precious; I could not just spend time together anymore or stay in the school building after classes. I needed to go back home and sleep so I could get up on time for work. I even recall one day, Jean complained about not seeing me at all and wondered if I still was attending ALCC. I told him I still went to school but since I did not get off work until three p.m., I could not get there early as I used to do to meet with him by the time, he was done with his morning classes. It was just impossible. Jean understood and did not make a big issue of that after I explained to him how things were going. He just advised me to not let my job's expectations overcome my school. I promised Jean that was not going to happen and that I still knew what I was doing. On the other hand, I had to make sure that my work schedule was not causing a gap of communication with my roommate Chris, as he sometimes would come back home with tickets for parties at his Brooklyn College and would ask that I go with him. Most nights, I was very tired, but I did not want to offend Chris and make him think that I was not interested in his invitations, so I would manage to get in the mood and be ready to party with him. I do not recall if Chris had a job that occupied his after-school time, but he got home at hours no earlier than mine after school. There were nights that we both felt so exhausted that we would just sleep or order a pizza, as neither of us could fix something to eat. I looked at myself as someone who was on his own trying to make a way out and maintain certain stability in his life.

I barely talked to my father or anybody back home. I did not have time anymore to purchase phone cards and call home. For me, I needed to become as independent as I could and leave to my father only the responsibility of paying my school tuition; the rest, I could take care of. I was proud of myself, and even though I was not living the easy life I thought of before coming to the States, I was having a decent one. I had my own cell phone and did not have to be home to make an important call if I needed to. I had my monthly Metro card and did not worry about going from one side to the other of New York City. I could look at a nice pair of shoes in a store and manage to get them on my next payday. Everything made more sense to me, as I could have what I needed because I worked. For a moment, my life seemed to resume itself in that reality of the situation. I felt like my dreams were just dreams and that I was now living the true life, just the way it was supposed to be. There was no more racing, and everybody around me was doing the same, so there were no more giants to be racing with. This whole situation made me realize how a set of events or a given situation could destabilize one's fundamental beliefs. It did not in fact take too much for me to move from the very ambitious, determined student who viewed his academic successes as the sole purpose of his sojourn in America, to the pragmatic man who now understood that all that mattered was to be able to pay his bills on time, maintain his status to avoid troubles with Immigration, and have financial stability. That is what I had turned into, but as God knew well how and when to turn things around in the life of his children, it had to take another set of events and circumstances to bring me back to reason and re-activate that dying flame inside of me, as I was beginning to lose it.

My session was over at ALCC, and I had to decide whether I would go for another three-month session or transfer to a college where I could begin taking my major courses and work toward a degree. Also, my father was beginning to ask me to tell him how school was going and what exact progress I was making since I had left. I found myself in a position where I could not really say anything about my academic progress. It seemed as if I had been sleeping for a long time and now was waking up to realize that I was missing everything. I had to do something. I had to decide and tell my father what I was going to do for the next semester. As I knew that I did not want to have to go sit for another three months in a classroom, learning English, I had to begin looking for a college in New York City where at least I could register and pursue my degree. There were a variety of colleges in New York City. I said to myself that I just needed to choose one that would be close to my place, and saying so, I thought about the City College of New York, which was between 132nd and 133rd Street on the West side of Harlem. I knew where the school was located because I used to pass it on my way to Emile's place.

I did not have time to waste anymore and so I went to the administration building at City College to get information about how and when to register. The feeling was great to be in a U.S. campus. There were students in every corner of the campus. It was the sort of atmosphere I needed to be in at that moment. I felt revived and ready to start school. When I got into the administrative building at City College, the pictures of the college's alumni struck me. There were photos of important personalities of Black history hanging in the front hall, where a desk was set for visitors to get information. I could recognize Dr. Martin Luther King, Jr. and Rosa Parks, a picture of her arrest after she had refused to give her seat to a White man, thus defying the law that later would cause the famous Montgomery Bus Boycott of that time. Another photo was one of Colin Powell, who was one of the first Black people, if not the first Black person, to hold the seat of Secretary of State for The United States of America. The room was full of emotions for me, and as I could remember my readings on Black history, I felt the need to hurry and find out when class started and what I needed to do.

One lady walked toward me and asked how she could help me. I told her I needed to register for classes. She asked if I had filled out an application yet for admission at City College. I replied that I did not, and before I tried to explain why I had not filled out an application, as I did not know I had to fill one, she quickly grabbed a sheet that showed directions to buildings in downtown Manhattan. I needed to go there to fill out a CUNY application, and only after I was accepted could I come to City College and register for classes. This was unexpected for me, especially when the lady added that I might not be able to register for that semester since the process of the application took about two to three months before I'd have an answer. I asked the lady if she really thought that I could not attend City College that semester. She replied with a nice expression from her face that she could not confirm that I would not be able to attend City College that semester, but that I really needed to hurry and get the application filled out at the CUNY Center downtown.

I understood that I had no time to waste there and decided to head to the CUNY Center, following the directions on the sheet she gave me. When I arrived at the CUNY Center after spending a long time in the train and having to cross through construction blockades to get to Manhattan. I asked one of the attendants in the room for an application for admission to City College. The gentleman was the one in charge of helping with such issues. He gave me a set of documents that I quickly began to fill out, writing down information about schools that I attended back home and the degree I received when graduating from high school. Another part asked that I talk about my personal ambitions and the things I wanted to do after I graduated from City College. I made sure I wrote down everything correctly and clearly so there could be no mistakes on the application. Then the man asked if I was an international student. I told him I was and he added that I needed to choose a date to take the TOELF exam required for candidates who did not have English as a first language. He also added that I could not be admitted to any CUNY institutions if I did not take the TOELF exam. So, it was mandatory for me to find a time as soon as possible to take that exam. I asked the man when the next exam was available. He told me the next exam was going to take place in the next two days and that if I missed it, I would have to wait for two months before I could take another one. In knew that I could not wait for another two months to take the test, so I decided to register for that one even if it meant that I was going to have to study my grammar and other reading materials in a limited period. I was confident and strongly believed that I could make it and receive a passing grade. The man handed me another sheet, which I had to fill out to be registered in his system for the coming exam. While he was entering my information in his computer, my attention was caught by a name on the list of those who had already registered for that same exam. It was the name of Jean Noel. I knew it was his because there could not be two with the same Gabonese name of Jean Noel in New York City. It had to be him. So, I decided that on my way back home, I would stop at Jean's place and verify what I saw.

I left the building after the man got everything set and gave me a card that looked like a Student ID, saying that I needed to present it the day I came for the exam, otherwise I would not have access to the room. I politely thanked the man and exited the building. On my way out, I thought that as tired as I was beginning to feel, I could not walk to the train station and wait, so I stopped a yellow cab in front of the CUNY Center building and asked to be taken to Jean's place. When I arrived at Jean's, I did not have to go to Emile's since I saw Jean from the window of his room. I called to him from where I stood at the entry and let him know I was there. He soon met me and we just sat out on the stairs, as I did not want to go in and spending more time. I told him about seeing his name at the CUNY Center. He reacted surprised and asked how that was possible. I told him that I went to register for the TOELF, as I was filling out an application to go to City College. He then admitted that he did register for the TOELF and was one his way to be accepted at another CUNY institution whose name I did not recall, but surely one in New York City. I told him I was so excited and that we needed to support each other during the exam. We talked about it while we sat outside enjoying the refreshing wind blowing on Amsterdam Avenue, mumbling over the rhythm of the Puerto Ricans' and Dominicans' Reggaetón sounds that almost dominated the whole neighborhood.

Then I left Jean and we reminded each other to make it on time to the CUNY Center the day of the exam. I warned Jean to not sleep too much that night and somehow forget to be there on time. We both laughed about it and I left. The night before the day of the exam, I watched the news and it was being said that the MTA workers were going to be on strike the next day for at least the first part of the day and possibly there was not going to be any train or bus in service, so people needed to decide how to get to their workplace on their own. The reporter, nevertheless, added that the information was not confirmed and that things may change in the next hours depending on the MTA worker's association and the resolutions they made with the mayor. That news was a little scary to me, as I did not know what I was going to do if there were not going to be any trains or busses in service. I called Jean that night and asked if he watched that information. Jean told me he just got it too and that certainly he was going to get a taxi to get downtown and walk to the CUNY Center. I told him I was going to do the same.

The next day I got up early as Chris was still sleeping. I made sure I did not make any brusque noise that could wake him up, and I fixed myself scrambled eggs for breakfast before I left the room. When I got in the street, I noticed that most people were walking and stopping cars to ask for a ride. It was unbelievable. The MTA strike was in fact in effect – and in a city like New York City, where most people depended on public transportation, it was horrible to see the crowd on the street. There were no empty taxis and I was beginning to worry about the whole situation. I needed to reach downtown as soon as possible and it was impossible to get a cab. After I walked about ten blocks, I finally got a taxi that could take me downtown. The traffic was rude on the way downtown and was really beginning to panic while sitting in the taxi. I could not allow myself to miss my exam, or else I would have to wait for another two months. When we arrived in the downtown area, I got off the cab and began running to reach the CUNY Center.

I was sweating when I entered the building and presented my card to the security guard in front of the round revolving door, I had to go through to get in. By the time I reached the room where the exam was going to take place, one lady walked toward me and told me I could not enter the room because the exam was already taking place and late participants were not allowed. I could not believe what I was hearing and I did not restrain myself from screaming at the lady that I needed to take that exam; otherwise, I could not attend school that semester. But all my efforts were in vain. The lady was clear and refused to understand anything that I tried to explain to her. I mentioned the MTA strike and the difficulties I had getting a taxi, but nothing worked for the lady. The rule was that no candidates should be allowed in the room after the test had begun no matter the reason. My whole body loosen like a boxer falling after having received a strong knock from his opponent. I did not know what to say after the lady left and made sure I understood that she could not let me in. What was I going to tell my father? What was I going to do that semester? So many questions began popping in my mind that I was struck by a sudden headache that only a deep sleep could relieve.

I decided to walk out of the building and get a taxi to head home because I could not stay there anymore; otherwise, I surely would lose my mind. When I got home, Chris was getting ready to leave for school. He noticed the look on my face, as I was so broken that there was no way, I could hide it. He asked what happened; I told him the whole story, and Chris felt so sad for me, he did not know what to tell me. I told him that I was going to be fine, that I just needed to sleep a little bit. I knew that Chris was not satisfied with what I told him, as he continued asking if I was sure I was going to be okay. I reassured him that he did not have to worry and that he could go to school and we would talk about it when he was back. He left the room and as he was locking the door, I lay down on my bed and felt my eyes closing. Sometimes when a given situation reached the extreme, the only way to seek a way out was to just sleep and hope that whenever you woke up, things would be different.

The whole situation was still puzzling my mind and I could not stop asking why this was happening to me. When I woke up after having slept for good hours, Chris had already returned from school and had been fixing something for us to have for dinner. He decided not to wake me up when he arrived, as he noticed that I was profoundly asleep. Finally, after he handed me a plate so I could serve myself, he brought up the subject, asking that I tell him what I was going to do next. I told Chris that I did not know what I was going to do and did not want to think about it. Chris did not seem to understand the depth of the situation and he tried to tell me not to take it too seriously because there certainly would be something that I could do to go to school that semester. I asked Chris what he thought I should do. Obviously, he did not have a clue about what I could do but he kept saying that I needed to try some other schools. I told Chris that if I were not going to be able to attend college that semester, I did not think I was going to anymore, as I did not know what my father would think about it. I somehow came to think that my father would not perceive the situation the way it happened but may think that I just voluntarily messed up and refused to go to school while he sent money for me to do so. It was going to be difficult to tell my father what happened, so I needed to find another alternative as soon as possible. Later, before Chris and I were done eating dinner, my phone rang and it was Jean. I first did not want to take his call because I was still upset and knew that he was going to ask me about the exam. But I finally decided to take the call, at least to inform Jean about what happened to me. When I told him that I had not even taken the exam, Jean could not believe it and first thought that I was kidding or something. I told him I was serious and that I surely was not going to be able to attend college that semester. Somehow, Jean did not find the situation as alarming as I thought he would. Instead, he laughed about it and told me he did not believe everything was done. I asked him what he meant or what he thought I could do. Jean was a very relaxed guy by nature and his attitude when I told him about what happened revealed his personality. He told me I could still go to college if I really wanted to, but it would have to be outside New York. At first, I felt very confused and thus asked him to make his point clear to me so I could hurry and do what I had to do. He told me that he was not going to attend a CUNY College because he had an admission letter to a community college in Texas. In fact, there was a college in Texas that he heard about from a friend of his who resided there and he did not need to take a TOEFL to be registered there. I insisted that he tell me about it and how I could contact that school. He told me the school's name was Grayson County College and it was in a small town in North Texas called Denison. I told Jean that we needed to meet the next day so I could call the college in Texas and find out what I needed to have ready to be registered. Before Jean hung up, he added that I should know about that college because most students who came to the States through Mrs. Dahir headed to Grayson after they spent a month at an ESL center, so I should call Mrs. Dahir and see if she could help me somehow. I thanked Jean for everything that he informed me about and really did not know before that what I could do.

Chris looked at me for a while and started laughing from his bed; he soon came over to mine and put his arm over my shoulder, saying that he knew that everything was going to be all right. He loudly laughed at the idea that I was going to go to Texas and leave New York City. I did not even want to talk about it that night since only the idea of going to school haunted my mind.

When I went to meet with Jean the next day, he was in his room and I noticed that he had started packing his stuff. I asked if he really was serious about going to Texas. He did not joke about it at all but let me know that he had already bought his ticket. I could not believe it until he showed it to me and I could see that he was not joking at all. I told Jean that I was going to send an email to Mrs. Dahir in which I would ask her to contact the advisor at Grayson so they knew that I would be going there for the semester. Jean had his laptop in his room, so from there, I sent an email to Mrs. Dahir, explaining the entire situation that I was in. I knew that Mrs. Dahir checked her email every single hour, as she remained connected twenty-four hours a day via the Internet. The next day, when I checked my mail via Jean's laptop, I found that Mrs. Dahir had already replied to my late message. She was asking me to call a lady whose name was Kathy Pearce. She was the international student advisor at Grayson County College and because Mrs. Dahir already sent her an email about me, she should be expecting me to call her. Mrs. Dahir added that she thought that I was already attending college and did not know what happened. I sent her another message in which I thanked her for everything and promised to remain in

93

touch with her more than I did before. Without wasting time, I also decided to call Kathy Pearce at Grayson County College since Mrs. Dahir made sure to send me her phone number. After the phone rang about two times, a strong woman's voice responded. The lady introduced herself as Kathy Pearce, the international student advisor at Grayson County College. I told her my name and before I even finished with it, she replied, saying that she had been expecting my call a little bit earlier, as she had received Mrs. Dahir's message about me. I told her I also just received her phone number and was ready to begin the admission process. She told me I needed to be in Texas as soon as possible because classes were starting in two weeks and I would need to make a reservation for a room in the school dormitory before the official date for the beginning of classes; otherwise, I would not have a room. I told Mrs. Pearce that I was going to be there by the end of the week and that I would have everything ready by the time I got there. The lady seemed genuinely nice over the phone, and I could already feel the excitement in me. Jean, after I ended the conversation with Mrs. Pearce, asked that I tell him what I really was going to do, because he was ready to leave and if I really meant to leave by the end of week, then we would leave together. He would just have to confirm his Greyhound ticket for the day we were going to depart. I told Jean that I would be ready to leave on Friday since it was a Wednesday morning that day. We had just one more day in New York City and had to pack everything for Friday. I knew that I had to call my father before I left New York because he needed to know where I was going to stay and what I was going to need when in Texas.

So, when I left Jean's room, I headed home and got myself a phone card on my way there. I called my father when I reached my room, and when he answered, I first asked how he was doing and how everybody else was doing back home since I had not talked to them for a while. He told me everybody was all right and that he worried about me since I was not calling at all. I told him I had been doing fine but was a little busy with my classes at the school of language and the little job that I was doing. I did not want to get into the details about it, so I straightly brought the subject to him by telling him that I was going to leave New York for Texas, where I was going to start college in two weeks. My father never showed that he was surprised about something at first impression. He just listened and asked if I had all the information, I needed to make sure I knew what I was doing. I told him I had already called the school and that they were expecting me to be there as soon as possible – and because I did not have time, I was going to leave on Friday. He told me it was too early for him to send me money to head to Texas. I told him that he did not need to send me the money to travel but he would just need to be ready for my tuition when I got to Texas. We finally concluded that I was going to send him my new address whenever I was in Texas so he could make a Western Union transfer for my tuition and the expenses the school would require. He added that he met with Aunt Suzanne and that they were going to have her at home for a family meal before she returned to the States. I told him that was going to be nice and that certainly Aunt Suzanne would appreciate that. Then we said good-bye and Dad wished me a safe trip, recommending me to the hands of the Lord. My father never finished a conversation with me without recommending that I pray to God all the time and walk in accordance with the angels he had sent to protect me wherever I was. That was his code of life, and I surely was not going to step out of that code which really was the foundation of our faith.

Now, I needed to begin packing my stuff and arranging for a transfer from ALCC to Grayson County College. I had to go meet with Mr. Octavio and let him know of my decision to head to Texas so he could officially proceed with my transfer. Because I did not have much time left, I decided to give Mr. Octavio a call and hope that we could talk about all that over the phone and I would know if I needed to meet with him in person or if it could be dealt with without requiring my presence at the school. I thought that by proceeding like that, I could save time and make sure all my things I had to take to Texas were ready. Mr. Octavio, after I explained to him what my plans were, he told me that he did not require me to physically be at ALCC for a transfer. I needed just to go to Texas and from there, my new advisor would have to send a transfer form that he would fax back to her with my Sevis information. This worked to my advantage so I thanked Mr. Octavio and told him I had enjoyed my time at ALCC and surely was ready for something else. He wished me good luck and suggested that I call him whenever I made it to Texas so he would know when to be expecting my transfer letter. The next thing I needed to do before the end of the day was inform Ruth at the restaurant about my transfer so she could pay me for the days I worked last. I left the apartment to make that trip from Harlem to Riverdale that had become my daily itinerary.

When I arrived at the restaurant on a day I was not expected to work, Ruth welcomed me in with a smile that was familiar to me. She asked what was going on and I told her that I was leaving New York the next day for Texas to continue my studies. For a moment, as I was explaining to her what trigged that whole situation, Ruth appeared very sad because she could not help keeping her happy humor, she held my hand and told me that she would not worry about me at all because she was sure that I was going to do great and that sometimes I will come back to visit her in New York City. I promised her that I would do so. Then she headed toward the counter and pulled out an envelope in which she had put my pay for the last days I worked. I did not want this to last forever so I excused myself to her and told her I had to leave. Before I exited the restaurant, I waved at Pedro from where he showed his head by the kitchen window, and with a sign of his hand, he wished me a safe trip.

Now that I had everything taken care of, I could go home and lie down for the night. On my way back to home from the train station at 125th Street, while we passed those streets and avenues, I had become so familiar with, I began to feel a little sadness within. It was as if again I was experiencing the exact same feelings, I had the night I left Gabon. After all, New York City had become my new home and I had learned so much living in New York that the idea of going to Texas became increasingly troubling to me. I did not know anybody in Texas and the only picture that I had about Texas was that image of cowboy's town where everybody wore a hat and rode a horse. I needed to learn more about this new place to which I was heading. So many questions began to pop up in my mind about the very lifestyle in Texas and how I was going to adapt to it. I was surely going to miss the MTA, the lights of Time Square, the Apollo Theatre that represented one iconic building in the history of Harlem. I mean these were things that eventually had become parts of my person, and now that I was spending my last night in New York City, they were all coming back to me in the form of souvenirs. It felt as if I would never come to New York again or at least for a long time – I could not really determine now. But I still said to myself that I did not have any other choice but to leave if I wanted to make my dream come true. Only the path of education could help me make it and therefore the good times in New York that I was going to surely miss, could not change my mind.

As I noticed that I still had hours, before it really got late, I decided to go to Emile's apartment and spend time with him and eventually I knew I would meet Jean there as well. Once at Emile's place, my feelings grew even stronger about the trip to Texas. Emile could not stop telling me how much I was going to miss New York and everybody else in there. He pointed out that for the time he had been in the States, he thought about leaving New York on occasions, but he never could make the final move because he was not sure he could fit in other states. I mean, we all had challenging times in New York City, but the city itself gave us hope of a better tomorrow and besides, living in New York City allowed us to feel in permanent contact with wherever each of us called home. Because Emile knew that I was not happy with what I had to do, he began to make it easy on me by telling jokes about what girls looked like in Texas. I asked him how he could talk about Texas girls when he never left New York. We all laughed about it and he continued to add that he was sure that I was going to find a good girl over there and that I just needed to speak French and they would love it. Well, that surely was not something unique to girls in Texas, not even in New York City, the French accent still was a powerful asset for girl-hunters. Jean joined us later and we shared drinks with Emile and another one of his friends whom I had not met before. He was called "Pouguy," and I could not stop laughing at his moves when dancing to the rhythm of Oliver Ngoma's song "Adia." I had never seen someone dancing as Pouguy was and I just wished that I had met with him before that night so he could have taught me his moves. The atmosphere was one of a last night of show time at Emile's place. We went downstairs to the convenience store every two hours to purchase more drinks, as the four of us in the room drank as ten. For hours, it was not anymore about going to miss anything in New York, but more about going to have amazing times in Texas. Emile even asked that we give him our addresses whenever we arrived there so he could see us sometime the next summer. Jean and I knew that there was no more staying in New York, but we were heading to Denison, Texas with our New York style. We tried to make fun of what other guys might look like in Texas and the picture was not one to stand with the one we had of ourselves. However, none that was serious as we just tried to feel comfortable and not let Emile's comments about New York City win us through.

After partying at Emile's for hours, I decided that I needed to leave the place and go home so I could rest for a while, even though we had already begun the first hours of Friday and therefore, I had just a few hours before we would head to the Greyhound Station. Jean agreed with that and we both said good-bye to Emile as he wished us to have a safe trip and make sure to give him a call when we arrived in Texas.

When I got home, Chris was deeply asleep, but I decided to wake him up so we could have fun and good moments to think about one another by the time I was gone. So, I began to sing in a very loud voice so he would wake up and wonder what was going on. I told him he should not be sleeping because his best roommate ever was leaving in few hours and wanted to have drinks with him. Chris did not really drink alcohol. He would just have one beer that he would not even be able to finish by the time I was on my third. So, we just sat there in the room, talking about Texas and how I was going to become a cowboy and ride horses to school and listen to old country music. Chris talked to me about Dallas, Texas and their basketball team called the Mavericks. I had no clue about that team, as I had never been a basketball fan. But Chris played and could talk about players from different teams, mentioning their names and where they came from, I mean, all that he knew about basketball. He told me that if he had to go to Texas, he would go to either Dallas or Houston. Honestly, before he mentioned these cities, I had had no clue about where they were and for what they were known. Well, I could say that when I heard about Dallas, I just recalled the TV show that was so famous all over the world with the Southern ranch. I knew nothing about Houston, so I began to ask him what he liked about Houston, a place he never went to before. Chris, compared to the things Emile said about Texas, knew what he was talking about even if he had never been to Texas, he was well informed about what it looked like over there. He told me President Bush was from Texas and that the famous actor Chuck Norris was from Texas and other celebrities that I had heard about but did not know where they lived in the U.S. He added that Dallas was the city where President Kennedy was shot; and that people flew from all over the world to Dallas, just to locate where that happened. Moreover, at least I had learned in very few hours, things about Texas that I did not know about. I thanked Chris for all that he told me about Texas and made sure he knew that I was going to miss his company. He replied by saying that I should not be speaking like so because we were still in the U.S. and that being in Texas was not the end of the world; we still could see each other whenever we decided to do so. Chris was right, and I realized after he said that, that I was still going to be in the United States and I still could go to New York whenever I wanted to. The conversation with Chris at that moment was allowing me to view my trip to Texas differently. Somehow, I had been viewing the trip as though leaving for another country and that it was going to be quite difficult for me to make it back to New York if I wanted to see my friends. It was not the case. I should not have been saddening myself with the things I was leaving in New York, because they were still going to be there and whenever I decided to go back, New York and its people was still going to be there. Suddenly, I felt as sober as if I had not even been drinking the whole night and without realizing it, the sun was already out and it was seven o'clock on Friday. I nevertheless felt sorry for Chris, because I kept him awake for the night while he had to go to school that morning. He was fine with that and just asked me to make the best of myself in Texas and make my dreams come true so we could hang out in New York City again with some of those luxurious vehicles we admired so much in downtown Manhattan, suggesting that their owners must surely be some lawyers or doctors – as many very important personalities one could count in New York City. I promised Chris that I was going to make it and that we would stay connected and hear from one another after I arrived in Texas.

Chris left for school, and I began putting my things together. I had to take a shower and look for a taxi to take me to Grand Central, where the Greyhound Main Station was in Downtown Manhattan. I had to make sure that I got there on time because Jean had mentioned to me that sometimes it would take hours standing in line before you could get to a cashier and purchase a fare ticket. So, I did not waste too much time at home and as soon as I was done in the shower, I got my clothes on and headed downstairs with my two bags, stopping a taxi that would drive me too Grand Central. When I arrived at the station, I started looking for Jean because while on my way there, I had called him to find out if he was there already. He told me he too was on his way and so whoever got there first needed to look and wait for the other. After a couple of minutes walking from one corner to the other, we both finally met at the main entrance. Jean looked ready to go. I could read the expression on his face. He wore blue jeans and one of those "I Love New York" T-shirts. I guess Jean had planned to make sure that when we arrived in Texas, everyone would notice that we came all the way from the Big Apple. He also had his ticket ready, for he got it a week ahead of me so he could benefit from a discount on the total cost of his fare. Mine was going to cost twice what Jean paid. I did not really have another option since I had not planned this trip. Just as Jean predicted, I stood in line to get to the cashier for about an hour before I could purchase my ticket. The Greyhound agent was a very nice-looking lady who was enjoying her job, as one could tell by her good manners, revealing her good customer service skills. When she asked for my ID and noticed what my name looked like, she gave me one of those beautiful smiles and asked where I was from. I asked her to give it a guess. To make it easy on her, I told her I was from Gabon and was heading to Texas. She added that she had never heard of that country before and she surely was going to read about it whenever she got off. I assured her that she would love all that she would find about Gabon and before I left her counter, I let her know that my accent was French. She seemed very attracted after I mentioned what my accent was, and while I joined Jean, I said to myself, surely Emile was right about the power of that French accent for lady hunters. The next step for Jean and I was to locate our bus number and the time scheduled for departure. We both needed to find the bus number 13, and as we walked in the station, following the numbers, we reached our waiting area. One could not tell at first sight where all those people were headed to because everybody still was looking for their bus number even when they stood in the room with the number 13 that indicated what the bus destination was. I still can see that gentleman walking toward Jean and me, asking where we were heading because he could not find his bus line. Jean showed the sign with a suite of numbers along the wall and told the man he just needed to look on his ticket and follow the numbers to locate his waiting room. Also, there were limited seats in the room so people laid their blankets on the ground and sat on them, others sat on their bags, while most people just stood up. I suggested to Jean that we needed to buy snacks and drinks for the road. I recalled that my father and I, whenever we drove from Libreville to the village, we would buy cookies and fill our bags with bottles of water and orange juice, as my father liked them so much. Jean agreed with that, so we got cans of coke from a vending machine and a couple of cookies. Since we could not find an unoccupied seat, we decided to stand just like most people and wait for the bus to arrive. Fortunately for us, we would not have to stand for a long time, because after a few minutes, our bus arrived and everybody was asked to line up at the entrance and hold their ticket to be handed to the Greyhound agent who stood by the door of entrance and tore off one part of the ticket's itinerary while handing the other part to the passengers. The room was agitated, and the more bus lines were being announced, the more people were rushing from one corner to the other, and Jean and I were pushed from one side to the other. It reminded me of my high school days when class was over and everyone rushed out through the door, trying to be the first to exit the room, for whatever reason I do not recall – but surely nothing that made sense, since we all ended up out of the classroom. It was the exact same situation in that room, and I told Jean that we did not need to rush at all because we had our tickets and that meant there were going to be seats for us even if we were the last to exit the room. Jean found that the situation was even funny and while people would rush through the door, we just took our time and let everyone pass us before we finally reached the agent who could not restrain himself from asking what Jean and I thought about all these people rushing to get on the bus. I told the man that surely the bus had comfortable seats in there and not so comfortable ones that everyone was trying to get and avoid. The man found it funny but agreed that they surely had their point in rushing out. We thanked the man after he handed us our tickets, and he wished us a safe trip to Texas. There we were, at the decisive point, ready to get into the bus and leave the ground of New York City. Jean and I looked back, before we made the first steps into the bus, trying to get a last image of the people in the station, and we were asked by the bus driver to walk in and find our seats. It was quite clear that everybody else had made their choice of seats they thought were good enough for them, and so the rest were left for Jean and me to sit on. We were at the very back of the bus and when we walked back there and I saw the proximity of our seats to the inside toilet of the bus, I told Jean that now I understood what everybody tried to avoid. Jean laughed about it and while we managed to get to our seats, the bus driver was ready to depart. As for myself, it was the beginning of a more personal journey, a journey that was going to determine another step in my life, a journey that resembled the second turn for an athlete required to make his third circle of the stadium to win the race. It was the beginning of my journey in Texas and only God knew what was going to happen to me in the pursuit of my dream at the end of that journey.

Texas

I have learned of my entire sojourn in Texas that beyond the moments of hardships, trials, and tribulations of any sort in the life of a man, there is a major teaching which at the end, would determine the true nature of these painful moments. Therefore, one should not break his mind lower in times of troubles but meditate and accept these moments as necessary in the fulfillment of his edification.

For those who have experienced a Greyhound road trip, especially when heading from the northern to the southern side of the United States, they certainly would have been chocked at some points by the sudden break from New York's skyrocketing buildings and Manhattan's lights which give it an air of a little "Eldorado" made of only light bubbles, to the open expression of America's natural view of mountains, hills, and plains where one could observe buffalo and horses in well-aligned farms. I could feel the change within, and the more we headed down south, the more I felt like I was losing something inside of me that was being replaced by something new which I could not yet determine the nature of. The sight was changing as we drove and headed down south, and I am sure even Jean could feel and see it too. It took us two days to arrive in Texas. Jean and I had the opportunity during that trip to admire the true beauty of America beyond life in the cities. I could not restrain myself from standing on my seat each time we crossed a bridge; the height did not only mesmerize me, but also by the beauty and aesthetic of the construction. I mean, I had never seen anything like those bridges before, and I could only think about my own country and dream that someday we would be able to build those kinds of edifices and have a better public transportation in Gabon. I could see and feel the American genius during that trip. On the second day of our road trip, it was around five p.m. when we arrived in a town called Sherman, Texas. It was in fact our destination. We got off the bus, tired and feeling filthy since we last showered in New York two days prior. The bus dropped us off at the Greyhound station in Sherman, which was a small room with a counter for the receptionist, one bench for passengers who waited to depart or be picked up, there was an aisle leading to the restrooms, and that it was about it to describe Sherman's bus station. It was the smallest Greyhound Station Jean and I had stopped at during the entire trip. I told Jean that certainly the size of that station revealed what the entire town was like. We laughed about it and got our bags off the bus; that one was heading back on the road to the city of Dallas, as we heard other passengers mentioning where they were headed. We made it to Texas safely, and from the depths of my heart, I thanked my God for it while Jean suggested calling his friend who should have been at the station by the time we arrived. I relied on Jean at that point because I did not know anybody in Texas except for Mrs. Pearce, whose number I had, but surely could not call to pick me up from the Greyhound Station. After a couple of minutes of trying to reach his friend, we saw a silver Ford driving toward the station and soon, parking before our bags. The driver got out and approached Jean and me, and just as if he knew, he greeted us in French and asked if we were waiting for Paskier. Jean told the guy that he was Paskier's friend from New York and that he had been trying to reach him but his phone did not ring at all. The guy replied that he was Ulrich and he was a friend of Paskier and because he had to work, Paskier could not make it to the station and therefore sent Ulrich to pick us up. Jean and I thanked Ulrich for coming and while we began taking our bags to Ulrich's car, I introduced myself to him as well. Trying to make it funny, I asked Ulrich about the population count in that town. He found it very funny and so before he could say anything, he laughed about it and asked if I also came from New York. I told him that I had lived in New York as well. That seemed to have been enough to help Ulrich make his point. He told me that I needed to ready myself to accept the tremendous change I was going to experience in Sherman, Texas. I did not get what Ulrich had in mind when he said that, but I understood that things were not going to be the same as they were in New York City, but how much worse they were going to get, I could not tell yet. Ulrich drove us away from the Greyhound Station to the main road, which he told us was called Texoma Parkway. This was the road that linked the city of Sherman to the city of Denison, where the college was located. I felt a little confused when Ulrich added that he attended Grayson County College as well but resided in Sherman. I could not figure out why he would live in Sherman and go to school in Denison. Wasn't there any college in Sherman for him to go to? But he quickly cut off my questioning by explaining that Grayson County College was the only school most residents of both cities could attend because the cost of tuition was affordable for everybody compared to another school in Sherman, which he called Austin College. He said that if he had been a rich kid, he surely would be attending Austin College, which according to him was mostly attended by well-off kids. After Ulrich told us about Austin College and Grayson County College, I could not wait to visit them both and see for myself what they looked like. We drove for about fifteen minutes before we entered an apartment complex named Parkview. It looked so nice outside and the apartments were so nicely built they gave me the impression of being in a very reserved residence where rich kids would reside. I then began to wonder what category of guy Jean's friend was if he was living in such a lovely place. Ulrich parked before one apartment and with a sign with his head, he let us know that we had arrived at our destination and could take our things from the trunk. Jean looked not very amazed by all this and I could not tell what exactly was on his mind, but I preferred to not ask him because I knew that he was going to let it out to me whenever he felt it appropriate to speak his mind as he always did. Ulrich rang the doorbell and someone came to open it. Ulrich greeted the guy at the door and told him he had newcomers for him; they both laughed for a moment at the door before the guy introduced himself as Igor welcomed us into his place. Jean and I both introduced ourselves to Igor and moved our things in. There was a guy in the room, and because he was focused on his video game, he barely looked at us until his part of the game was over. He finally approached Jean and me from where we sat, and while apologizing for not meeting us a minute ago, he introduced himself as X. Igor's apartment was very nicely equipped for a student's place and I would admit that I said to myself that Igor's parents must be some very important personalities in Gabon to let him live in such a comfort. I mean, I could see his apartment and compare it with my place in New York City, and there absolutely was no match at all. I do not even know why they called it an apartment; to me, it was more of what could be a house in Gabon – and not one of a college student. I began to somehow understand the kind of change Ulrich told me I needed to prepare myself to experience. There was a huge flat screen TV, which connected with his video game, a pile of DVDs and CDs, and all kinds of electronic devices. The couch where we sat was also not a cheap one, and even though I tried to not think about all those things, I could not remain indifferent. I was trying to understand how – in a small town like that one, Igor could live in such luxury; when I lived in New York City, I could not even get close to living in such an apartment while still in college. The answer certainly was going to come to me with time and experience, I said to myself. I was nevertheless able to distinguish one key point of contrast between Southern lifestyle and Northern accommodation. It seemed to me easier to have a comfortable home in the South than it was in the North and this eventually was evidence for one to consider when moving from one side to the other. In fact, it did not take me long to begin considering the potential changes I was going to go through in Texas. We stayed at Igor's apartment for about an hour, talking about anything and everything, just as normal people do to get to know each other better. Igor had been attending Grayson County College for two semesters and was pursuing an associate degree in biology. His friend X was a computer major and it really was his passion as he accounted to us his years of studying computer programming at Omar Bongo Technical University in Gabon, which is the country's first technical school. I personally could value his technical skills in the field, because I have a brother back home who attended the same university and was good with computers. Jean told the guys that he was going to major in geology and this because of his love for rocks and the study of the underground. It was uncommon, not only for me, but for Igor and X too, to hear that a Gabonese student was interested in the study of rocks, but there was Jean – and we could just encourage him and wish him well in his pursuit. Then I told the guys that I opted to major in political science and international relations. I still remember the expression on my friend's face after I said it. Igor laughed and, ironically as I felt it, he told me that if I made it, I surely was going to be Gabon's next Minister of Foreign Affairs. I found it very funny too and we all shared the joke. Then, I told the guys that I could speak English, Spanish, French, and German. That was another strike to the guys and now, Igor could not hold himself from his seat. He jumped over to me and grabbed my hand, shaking it to show his excitement, as he had never been closer to someone who could speak several languages. I assured Igor that just as X had a passion for computers, I spent my time learning other languages. For a while, we continued to talk about what our aspirations were and what we wanted to do for our country when we are done with school in America. The moment was so relaxing for us that we did not even notice how late it was and Paskier still was not there. I asked Jean if he had an idea of where Paskier could be since I needed to find out where we were to spend the night. It did not take long after we thought about trying another call, and someone knocked the door. It was Paskier. He came in with a big smile; at seeing Jean, they hugged one another and for a minute could not let go. This helped me determine how happy they both really were to meet again. In fact, Paskier and Jean had attended Leon Mba High School in Libreville and after they graduated, each one went his own way and did not hear from one another for long time. Paskier moved to the States a year before Jean did and he was in his last semester at Grayson. He seemed like a cool guy to me even though we did not actually talk after we introduced ourselves. He told us he had to work extra hours and that justified why he was not able to pick us up from the Greyhound Station. I told Paskier that I profoundly appreciated his help and would always be grateful for that. He simply smiled and told me I surely did not have to thank him at all, because I, too would have done the same for him. I agreed with that, and as everyone else seemed to be focusing on the two of us, I asked Igor if he did not have anything to offer his guests for the night just the way we did back home. It came out very amusing to the guys and Igor responded that he surely could offer me a piece of pizza as a welcoming food in his home. We all laughed after that and still, I walked to his kitchen and grabbed a piece of pizza from the counter. I had not eaten since our last stop at the Greyhound Station in Saint Louis where Jean and I walked to a McDonald's and got burgers. I was hungry and that piece of pizza surely was not going to be enough to cut my appetite. Jean did not seem to be sharing my hunger so he let me have the entire piece of pizza after I suggested that he shared it with me.

Because it really was getting late and Paskier surely did not want to keep Igor up that long, he suggested that we leave. Jean and I agreed with him, and by the time I got up to grab my bags from one corner of the room next to Igor's seat, Igor suggested that I stay with him while Jean went with Paskier. First, I did not know what to say and then, Paskier replied that the idea was fine with him, since he only had a two-bedroom apartment that he shared with one guy already and surely was going to share his bed with Jean for a while. So, Igor's suggestion was in fact welcomed. As both Igor and Paskier asked what I thought, I told them it did not matter if I stayed with Igor at all if I could have another piece of pizza. We all laughed on that one and everyone agreed that I spend the night at Igor's apartment and we should meet the next day and head to Grayson County College. Before they both exited the room, Jean joined me as I managed to get my things in Igor's bedroom. He asked if I was okay with staying at Igor's. I told him it was fine with me and that I did not see any reason to be uncomfortable. Jean tried to make sure that I was not feeling left out after he met with Paskier, but I assured him that he did not have to worry about anything because I was fine with it. Then he left and we promised to meet the next day. After everybody else left Igor's apartment, I wanted to take a shower before going to bed and Igor managed to show me where the bathroom was and all that I could use in there. I thanked him for his kindness and as I gathered my shower items, Igor asked me what made me decide to come to Sherman, Texas. Because I did not want to get into all the details with someone I barely knew, I just told him that I was interested in the affordable tuition that Grayson offered compared to most schools in New York City. He did not ask for much after I told him that, and I headed to the shower. Igor still lay on his couch, playing his video game by the time I was done showering. As I really began to feel sleepy and exhausted from the two-day trip, I told Igor that I was going to bed and I would see him the next day. He barely responded, as he was focused on his game, but I understood that he already got it before I told him. It did not take time for me to get into a deep sleep after I fell on Igor's bed. When I woke up the next day, I was surprised to notice that I was alone in the room. I got up from the bed and walked in the living room to check on Igor, but there was no one in the main room either. I began to question the situation within and wonder why Igor would not spend the night in his apartment when he had someone there, he barely knew. As I walked back in the bedroom, I noticed that the closet in which I put my bags was barely opened and from there I could perceive a human hand. I pulled the closet's door open and at my grand surprise, I saw Igor sleeping on a mattress, which I guessed he had arranged there for the night. I did not want to wake him up, as I believed that he must of have stayed up hours after I went to sleep and was trying to enjoy his sleep there in the closet. However, the whole situation was funny to me and as I got into the shower, I kept asking myself, why would someone go put a mattress in a closet and spend the night in there when there is a whole huge bed for two in the room. Again, I said to myself, certainly it was the kind of change I was going to experience in Texas. Igor did not have a car, as I was able to notice through the parking lot, which had reserved spots for every tenant in the complex. It was almost nine in the morning and Jean still was not there. I thought about giving him a call, but I soon realized that my phone was off as the battery had died. I needed to go through all my bags and locate the charger. As I was trying to make as little noise as possible to not disturb Igor's sleep, he suddenly got out of the closet and asked if I had had a good night. I told him I did sleep great and that when I woke up, I looked for him before I figured out that he was in the closet. He smiled when I told him about it and headed to the bathroom as I continued to look for my phone charger. Jean and Paskier were on their way to our place and so when I had my phone back on and tried to reach Jean, I noticed that he had sent me a text message, stating that he was on his way and that I needed to be ready by the time they got there because Paskier was going to head to work after dropping us off at Grayson. Soon, after I checked on Jean's message, someone was knocking at the door and when I walked by to see who it was, I saw Paskier from the window, standing by his car, which was a white Ford Focus. I then knew that it was Jean at the door. So, I opened and there he was all dressed up for the first day at Grayson County College. We hugged each other and he asked if I was ready to go. I told him that I was almost done and needed just to get my transcripts and we could leave. In fact, I just needed to grab my school bag in which I had always kept ordered all my academic documents. Igor came out from the room by the time Jean and I were leaving, and he told us he was going to meet us there in a couple of hours. Then, we left with Paskier and as we drove through the complex Igor lived in, to reach the main road, I noticed other cars behind us and it seemed to me that the people inside those cars were African students as far as I could tell, just by looking at them. I asked Paskier if there were other Gabonese students living there. He answered, telling me that he as well used to live there before he moved to his new place about six months ago. He added that there were about six Gabonese students in the complex and that we were going to meet them all on campus at Grayson country college. After Paskier explained that to me, I began to picture the student atmosphere at Grayson County College and it seemed to me that there might be a whole lot of French speaking students at the campus and therefore, there surely would be some little groups gathering of friends and relatives talking about everything and anything as the semester started. I loved the picture I was making in my mind and I really felt excited about being there already. After about fifteen minutes driving, we arrived at Grayson County College and I could see that huge banner on which was written in capital letters "Welcome to Grayson County College." I felt a little chilled and I could feel goose bumps up my arms. Here I was getting into an American campus, just like they were pictured in most movies involving American college campuses. The parking lot was as huge as the entire school itself. There were cars of different models everywhere, from old but renovated Toyotas to brand new types of cars. Jean Looked back at me and asked if I felt the same as he did. I told him I knew what he felt and I felt the exact same thing. While looking for an empty spot for him to park, Paskier smiled and asked if we were all right. Jean and I both looked at him and asked him how else we could feel when experiencing such a moment. "Welcome to Texas," Paskier said as he stopped his car and got out. Jean and I followed him and made sure we locked the doors behind us. Grayson County College was composed of six main buildings, as I could look at them while walking behind Paskier, heading to an aisle between two main buildings. Most buildings were newly built, and one could tell by comparing walls that appeared new to others that stood strongly and beautifully rebuilt to a more modern standard. Paskier walked us through the library, which also appeared renovated with two floors, one being the main entrance divided into a books department and a computer aisle, while the other one on the second level included classrooms and a department for artistic expositions. As we passed through the library, Paskier pointed to another building that included the cafeteria where most students who lived on campus enjoyed their breakfast, lunch, and dinner. I could smell the mixture of condiments coming from the cafeteria and as we passed it; I told Jean, we should stop there on our way back from the advisor's office. Jean found it very funny so he just gave me a quick smile after that. We were now getting to a quiet small office compared to the ones we passed on the way. It was Mrs. Pearce's office. One could not miss it and I would even say that Mrs. Pearce had organized everything in that office so that one knew at first who she was and who she took care of. There were drawings on each one of the walls. Someone had drawn a huge map of the African continent and colored most countries to identify where they came from. Also, there was a big round table in a little room that was a sort of waiting area for people who wished to meet with the advisor. We were not the only students in the room as we got in. There were about five to six other African students in the room and among those, there were three I could tell were from Gabon. Paskier walked us through in the little waiting room where the other students sat. Among the three Gabonese students in the room, I crossed eyes with one girl whose face was familiar to me. It seemed to me that I had met her before and surely it had been in Gabon. I could not yet determine where exactly, but I was certain she also felt the same. So, when Paskier introduced Jean and me to everybody else in the room, I asked the girl if we had not met before. She agreed that we surely had met somewhere. Then I asked where she went to high school back home because I was certain that if we did in fact meet back home, it must have been during an academic event. After she told me she attended Notre Dame de Quaben, a well-accredited Catholic school in Libreville, the one that my twin sister attended, I told her it was there that we had met. She asked if I was not involved in English activities in Libreville. I saw that she was getting close to it, so I made it easier by telling her that I was the President of the Martin Luther King, Jr. English Club, and that we had met during an all-school event that was organized by her school's faculty and that during that event, she helped organize seats for the many students who were hosted by Notre Dame de Quaben. She told me her name was Catherine but most people called her Cathy. I told her she could call me Frank but also Tucker if she wanted to. Then, we talked about other things for a couple of minutes, as Jean and Paskier discussed with the others in the room. After we waited for about an hour, a woman walked in the room and interrupted all the talks that were going on in the little room; she asked with a very sounding voice, "Who is Frank Tucker?" I stood up and told her I was Frank Tucker. She quickly walked to me and gave me a deep hug, one of the kinds of hugs I only saw people giving in Harlem.

"Hello Baba!" I said "Hello" back, and she asked who else had come along with me. Jean stood up and she did the exact same thing to him. Mrs. Pearce was in her fifties and she did not look like it at all. One could feel the joy and the strong energy coming out of every single one of her movements. She welcomed Jean and me to Grayson County College and walked both of us toward her desk. Mrs. Pearce's desk was nothing different from Mrs. Dahir's. You could tell how busy that woman was. She had to take care of every single international student on the campus, and each one had different situations or issues that she had to deal with. Behind the desk, there was a huge shelf, filled with folders and English books, and training manuals for the TOELF exam, required non-English speaking students. I imagined that Mrs. Pearce also taught English classes to international students. Jean and I sat on the other side of the desk as Mrs. Pearce was filling out documents that I assumed to be parts of our folders. Then, she asked how we felt about being in Sherman, Texas. Jean responded first and told her that he thought Sherman was a delightful place to live as a student compared to New York City where we came from. Mrs. Pearce agreed with Jean and she even added that she had a daughter who lived in New York City and that she had been inviting her to visit, but she never could find a time to make it to New York and she just wished she could make it sometime soon. I felt like I did not have anything to add to that, since I shared Jean's opinion and therefore just agreed with Mrs. Pearce's comment as well. She nevertheless asked what I personally felt. I smiled a little bit and in a very articulate way, I told her that I felt ready for the different lifestyle and that so far, I liked the place. After I responded to her, Mrs. Pearce stopped writing for a moment and stared at me with a questioning expression. Then she asked where I had picked up my English because to her, I was very fluent and she barely could tell that I was from Gabon. I looked at Jean and he too looked at me and we both began to laugh about it. Mrs. Pearce stopped us from laughing and asked again, looking serious about it. I told her that I did in fact speak English before I moved to the States and that from my early years in high school, I was an active member in an English club that had marked my first path in the study of Shakespeare's language. She was satisfied with my answer, and as she continued to fill out documents, I asked Jean if he too could not tell I was from Gabon. Jean nodded and smiled, letting me know what he thought about my English. In fact, from the time we first met in New York, Jean had told me that he believed I should not be taking classes at ALCC anymore because I already had the level needed for college. So, he knew that I had a good knowledge of English and I could already speak fluently while engaging in a talk. Mrs. Pearce asked if I had brought with me my transcripts; I pulled them out from my bag and handed them over to her. She made copies of every document I handed to her and returned to me the originals. She insisted that I keep all my school documents and identification very safe because they would go along with me, during my entire sojourn in the United States. I assured her that I always made sure to keep all my important documents in a safe place and ready to take out when needed. She said the same to Jean, as he handed to her his transcripts as well. She entered the information she could get from the documents we handed over to her into her computer system and she explained to us that she had to send our records to Immigration Services because as students on F-1 Visa, which is the term used to identify someone who entered the U.S. as a student, we were required to remain in contact with U.S. Immigration Services so that they could keep track of all that we do while in the country. She talked to us about a couple of other requirements I had not heard of before because I had not had a complete conversation with the advisors from ELS to ALCC about Immigration and ties international students had to keep with them. I would even say that of all the time I had spent in New York City, I had no clue what the word immigration stood for and how I was particularly bound to it. The last time I heard about it was when Mr. Octavio explained to me that I needed to have a certain amount of money to prove I was financially independent and could pay my tuition always before I could be issued an I-20. In fact, I thought of Immigration as a service that issued I-20s to foreign students and only that. Now Mrs. Pearce was informing us about an even deeper role of the Immigration services. They could decide of whether we could stay in the States or had to leave the country, depending on how well one maintained his fulltime student status. Mrs. Pearce talked to us about Grayson County College in general as she pointed out that the college had two main campus houses for on-campus students and that Jean and I were going to stay on the west campus called Jensen Dorm. There, most international students shared rooms with at least one native English-speaking students who were theatre majors, for the most part and were encouraged to live on campus so they could have quick access to performances and acting activities. Jensen Dorm also housed foreign students from different countries, mostly enrolled as international students. The other dorm was located on the main campus and was called Vikings Dorm. There resided the whole basketball team of Grayson County College. Choice was made because of the proximity to the gym, a necessary amenity for student- athletes. Mrs. Pearce added that there also were foreign students occupying rooms in the Vikings Dorm, but mostly because they were no more rooms available in Jensen by the time they enrolled. She also told us about the shuttle bus that left the main campus to pick up students at Jensen and take them back every two hours and we just needed to be at the bus stop whenever we had to head to Jensen or go to the main campus. It sounded fine to me, as I could at least still ride on a bus, something that reminded me of my New York daily motion. After Mrs. Pearce told us about the college and the things we needed to know about Immigration and international students, she asked whether we wanted to register at that moment or if we were going to wait and if so, we would be charged a late registration fee on the total amount of our tuition for the semester. I told her I had nothing to wait for and if I could right at that moment register and find out what I had to pay; I was ready to do so. Jean agreed with me about that and as he was on a government scholarship, he did not have to worry about anything at all. He just needed to pick his classes for the semester and register while Mrs. Pearce just had to put his bill on his scholarship and everything was done. When Jean told her that he was on a government scholarship, she smiled and in a very humoristic manner, told him that there were many students from Gabon on campus and most of them were on government scholarships and she just wanted to know what sort of rich country in Africa would grant scholarships to most students who went to study in the U.S. I personally felt a little stoked from within when she said that – not because her question was not appropriate, but more so because I knew that my country in fact did have the ability to grant scholarships to most Gabonese students studying abroad, but this was done in respect of some very unethical criteria. I barely could accept the fact that there were many Gabonese students at Grayson County College whose tuitions were on scholarships, so they just had to worry about studying and making good grades while I was going to have my parents struggle to pay for my tuition, when I knew that I deserved to have a scholarship, too. I could not talk to Mrs. Pearce about it at that moment and preferred just to listen and wait

117

for her to present to us the catalogue of classes available for the semester. Mrs. Pearce was like Mrs. Dahir except Mrs. Dahir was older, but their working habits were quite the same. Mrs. Peace seemed to always have something going on around her; she would take a call, talk for a minute, and by the time she hung up the phone, another call would come in and she just kept going. Jean and I would look at each other and wonder if she ever had a time to rest with all those calls. She finally pulled out a sheet from her drawer and explained that first, we both needed to register for a test she called Compass. It was a campus-administered test that would help determine not only our English level, but also our math skills. Mrs. Pearce explained that degree programs required a certain level of English before a student could register for it and the Compass was going to determine which classes Jean and I could register for. Jean asked when it was possible to take the test, and Mrs. Pearce answered that she was registering both of us to go take the test right away. "What!" Jean and I shouted at the same time. How was that even possible? We had barely studied anything. Mrs. Pearce did not seem bothered at all with our reaction, instead, she calmly added that we just needed to go to the testing center and present our identification cards, which at that moment were our passports, and tell whoever we met there that she sent us for the Compass test. Then she handed an information sheet to me and another one to Jean, explaining that we needed to print our name, address, and selected majors before turning them in to an advisor in the testing center. That was it for the moment with Mrs. Pearce, and before Jean and I walked out and went to the testing center, she held us both, putting her arms on our shoulders and shouting, "Go get me As and come back to finish your registration. Jean and I left Mrs. Pearce's office and joined Paskier in the other room. After Jean explained to him what Mrs. Pearce told us and what we needed to do that day, Paskier let us know that he had to go to work, so we would just have to stay on campus and look for someone to give us a ride home after we were done with the testing. Jean and I made it quite easy on Paskier, so we agreed and told him to have his phone on whenever he got off work, just in case we were not able to find a ride home. He assured us that he would do so, then left. Jean and I had to locate the testing center and go take the Compass. The testing room was not actually far from Mrs. Pearce's office, for it was in the same building and we just needed to walk past a couple of classrooms. We finally made it there, and as we entered the room, there was a huge sign hung on the main door that said, "Be silent in the study room." A blonde lady walked toward us and asked how she could help us. I responded that Mrs. Pearce sent us to take the Compass test and take the results to her so we could register from the semester. The lady kindly asked that we follow her to her desk, where she had us fill out a sheet with our names and basic information about any need each of us had to comfortably take the test. Then she asked that we show our identification cards so she could write us down on the list for the test. After we got done with the entire process to be administered the test, she walked us into the testing room where each of us had to sit before a computer. I asked the lady if the test was a computerized one; she affirmed that it was. I felt a little uncomfortable because I really had never take an exam of that kind via a computer and I barely could remember the computer class we had at ESL which was based on very elementary notions on how to start a computer, shut it off, and so forth. The lady felt that I turned a little cold when she put me in front of the computer, so she added as to assure me that there was nothing difficult about taking the computerized test because everything was self-explanatory; I just had to read and cross the right answer. She also added that most questions were multiple choice and should be easy for us to get through. After she made it clear to me, I felt more at ease and ready to begin my test. Jean sat before a computer in the second row ahead of me, so we could not really talk to each other as he had his back turned to me and the lady made it clear that communications were not allowed in the testing room. However, before I started my test, I wished good luck to Jean and he did the same. The test had three main parts that I had to get through before it was all over. The time was unlimited, so I could stay there if I wanted to and therefore did not have the pressure of running out of time. There were questions on reading, writing, and algebra. Because I had not always been a good student in math, I decided to spend my time on the reading and writing parts, as I knew that I was not going to do well in math. Jean and I sat there in the room for over two hours and after struggling with my algebra, I decided to end the test. I called in the lady and she walked over my desk, asked me if I had not done well. I told her I thought I did my best. She smiled and asked that I go wait for her by her desk, as she was going to print out my results. Jean as well was done and joined me in the room as we both waited on the lady to show us how we did. When she joined us, she seemed quite happy, so Jean and I told ourselves that we had done well on the test. Mrs. Thompson handed each of us a sheet, explaining that I passed one subject and failed the two others, while Jean passed his math and his reading but failed his writing, which I had passed. We had to then take the documents to Mrs. Pearce, who was going to help us enroll in those classes we had to take for the semester. Although I felt disappointed with my results, I also thought that I should not make a big issue of it since I was going to take a class that would help me better my reading and eventually continue to struggle with my math. We left the testing center and returned to Mrs. Pearce's office. By the time we got there, she was not in and so we had to wait in the little room where everyone had to stay when she was absent from her desk. After Jean and I sat there for less than an hour, Mrs. Pearce came in and I seriously would say that Kathy Pearce had so much energy that one could feel it coming through her voice. Jean and I walked to her desk so we could present to her our test results. "Hey, my babies," she said as we stood before her. She asked how the test was and if we got A grades. I looked at Jean and he looked back at me, and we both began to laugh about it. Then, we both handed our test sheets to her. She looked over both documents for few minutes, and then asked that Jean and I take a seat while she figured out what classes were available for us to register for. She flipped a couple of pages from a booklet on her desk and then checked courses I imagined were still available and corresponded to what Jean and I needed for the semester. Then, she handed me a printed document with my class schedule on it, while she handed another to Jean. She wanted to make sure that we could locate our classrooms. Grayson County College was not a noticeably big campus, though most buildings were spread out in different corners of the campus. So, it really was not going to be a major problem for Jean and me to find our classes. The next thing Mrs. Pearce made sure to discuss with us before she let us leave her office was what she presented as the need for both of us to live on campus for the first semester. I really did not know what Jean thought about that, but I personally was expecting to live on campus, at least for my first semester. Mrs. Pearce talked to us about the cost of tuition, including an on-campus stay and what the cost would be if we stayed off campus. Eventually it was more expensive living on campus than residing off campus. I did not have a choice, anyway since I did not really know where I was going to stay if I chose to live off campus, so I agreed that I would pay for my tuition and stay on campus. Jean decided not to say anything about it now and just let Mrs. Pearce know that he was going to think about it and let her know the next day. She seemed fine with it and so told us that she was through with us for the day and that we were free to leave whenever we wanted to. Jean and I thanked Mrs. Pearce and left her office while promising to see her the next day to finalize the registration process. As we exited the room, Jean winked at me and asked if I really wanted to stay on campus and pay all the money that was required for it. I told him I really did not have a choice, since I did not know anybody in Sherman and I could not just see someone and ask if I could stay with them. Then I asked what he was going to do. He answered that he had already arranged with Paskier, and he agreed to have him stay with him for the semester and hoped that he could find his own place by the time school was over. I told him I was happy for him, especially because he was going to save money by staying with Paskier. As we walked along one building that ran along the cafeteria, I asked Jean if we should not go in and get something to eat while we figured out how we were going to get home. Jean did not seem really interested with that idea and so he replied that if I really were hungry, we could get something to eat. He did not really want to go in there, and I could see that too. Plus, he added that most students who ate in the cafeteria lived on campus and he did not really want people to stare at us as strangers in the room. I told my friend that if he felt that way, we did not have to go in, and we could always try it another day. We continued to walk along the building, until we reached the library and noticed more African students as they spoke in their native tongues, and also in French. There was not anyone that either Jean or I knew to join and chat with in that room. I asked Jean if he felt that it might not be easy for us to make any friends if everyone spoke their own languages, and no one seemed to have noticed us in the room. Regardless, I walked toward three guys who seemed cool, one of them looked my way and with a sign of his head, he let the others know that I was coming to meet them. I greeted them all and introduced myself as new to campus, and because of that particularly, I needed to meet with those who had been attending Grayson before me. The three of them smiled at me and individually began to introduce themselves. One was Almami and was from Guinea; the other was Guy Patrick from Gabon – he would soon play a significant role in my growth process, and the publishing of this book, and finally Emmanuel from Cameroon. The three of them had been attending Grayson only for a semester and so did not consider themselves what I could label as campus veterans. Guy Patrick was a short guy of the body-builder type, and one could at first sight believe that he surely spent hours at the gym, growing muscles, and physical strength. Almami's physical appearance really could not hide that he was from Guinea, as most people of Guinean origins stood with that tall-but-thin body type. I could not say much about Emanuel, he just looked like a nice guy. Guy Patrick told me I was welcomed among them and that he did not believe there really was much they could tell me about Grayson College, other than I just needed to focus on my studies and make the best of myself everyday so I could finish fast and head somewhere else. While Guy Patrick shared with me what he thought, I could read in the eyes of Emanuel a sense of wanting to add something to what Guy Patrick told me. It seemed as if Guy was not telling me about something that Emanuel believed I should also be aware of. So, by the time Guy was done talking to me, I turned myself toward Emanuel and in a very humoristic way, asked if he did not have a little secret to share with me so my sojourn in Sherman, Texas could be of the most enjoyable. Emanuel looked at Almani and Guy Patrick, who like me, seemed a little puzzled about that look from Emanuel. Then he asked where I was going to stay. I answered that I was going to stay on campus for the semester, as I did not know anybody to stay with off-campus. Emanuel told me that I made the right decision because living off-campus in Sherman was not as easy as it seemed. I did not know what he had in mind, so I asked that he narrow that for me. Then he began talking about the necessity in Sherman for everyone to have his or her own car for transportation because the city did not have a public transportation shuttle and not everyone could afford to purchase a car. When Emanuel put that out, Guy Patrick automatically agreed with a nod of his head, just to make me understand how serious this matter was in Sherman. I guess, because I knew I would be living on-campus, and ultimately the lack of a personal car won't bother me that much, at that moment Emanuel's concerns weren't sinking in. As we stood there in front of the library, talking about life in Sherman, Texas from my three comrades standpoint and perspectives, Jean joined us and while he was introducing himself to the guys, I made sure that they all knew that he was my friend from New York and that we made the trip together to Sherman. Everything went well with our new friends and I somehow began to feel more comfortable about moving to Texas. In fact, I had a gut feeling that I was going to experience and learn from my stay in Sherman, although I also was a little anxious because I could not yet really determine the nature of what was to come. By the time everybody was leaving the campus, I decided that I was going to ask among my new friends for a ride to Igor's apartment. I wanted to ask Guy Patrick first, and luckily for me, he agreed to take Jean and me to Igor's apartment for he resided at the very same complex. The three of us then walked from the front of the library to the main parking lot toward Guy's vehicle. He had a black Taurus with four doors and leather seats. Jean and I were overly impressed but decided not to show it then, since, most students who attended Grayson County College seemed to have not only apartments of their own, but also their own vehicles, which was not the case in New York City, at least for those we knew. It really was an important shift for Jean and me, but at the same time, I could not get over the idea that there might have been a catch behind all this. It seemed too good, too easy for even African students who I knew mostly shared the same difficulties, to just be there, buy their own cars, and live in well-furnished apartments while attending Grayson County College. My friend Jean didn't really seem preoccupied by those questions. He behaved as if everything was normal, as if he already knew what the catch was in Sherman. Sometimes, when I told him that I was impressed about something I had found out about our friends' living style in Sherman, he would just laugh and play as if he could not believe I was ever impressed with that. As Guy drove us to Fairview Apartments, I had a better view of the town because he did not rush at all and took the time to show us the main stores and eating joints of Sherman. We drove past a huge parking lot, almost filled with cars, in front of a very nice-looking building with white and blue paint all around. Guy told us it was Wal-Mart, one of the major grocery stores and multi-shopping departments of Sherman. I had never seen or visited a Wal-Mart before and when Guy asked if there was one in New York City, I told him that I was not sure and that if there really was one there, I could not understand why I had never seen it. Jean added that he was not sure about having visited a Wal-Mart during his entire stay in New York City. That sounded somehow funny to Guy but he managed not to say it was. Then we drove by a couple of restaurants and fast-food places; I already knew McDonald, Burger King, and Jalapeno, which served Mexican food, and others. We finally reached the main gate at Fairview Apartments, where a huge sign was plugged in, welcoming everyone who entered the complex. Igor's apartment was about one block from the office so we did not drive too long before Guy reached our destination. Jean was going to stay with me at Igor's apartment and wait for Paskier to get off work so he could come pick him up. We both thanked Guy Patrick and promised to visit his place after we were all set with our final residences. It was about five p.m. – I had not really eaten anything for the day and my stomach was beginning to make its mandatory call. After I knocked on Igor's door and let him know it was me out there, he opened and with his incredibly quiet humor, asked how the day was for us at Grayson. I told him everything went fast and that Jean and I had to take the Compass that very same day; otherwise, we could not register at all for the semester. Igor shared with us that he, too had to do the same when he arrived at Grayson and that he did not understand why they kept doing that to us. We discussed it for a while, each of us giving his opinion and hoping to find why it was that we had to go through a test unprepared when we knew that the results of that test would determine what classes we could be registered for. It finally came to be about money for the three of us, because eventually the more classes you took, the more money you had to pay, and if you could be required to take some classes to take others, it became obvious that you would be bringing more into the college's financial gain. Another fact was because we were international students, we paid double the general amount for tuition, plus we were required to enroll in a minimum of twelve credit hours every semester; otherwise, we would lose our status and exposed ourselves to immigration penalties. None of us wished to be called by Immigration Services to respond to these sorts of issues.

I admitted that I needed to go to Grayson County College to better understand the picture given to the U.S. immigration services by most immigrants, especially people who entered the country on a Visa, but also unauthorized immigrants who arrived in the country via non-legal ways. In fact, the sojourn at Grayson opened my eyes to how important of an issue maintaining good standards with Immigration Services was for all international students. Jean and I stayed with Igor for a couple of hours before Paskier called on Igor's cell phone and checked with him to see whether Jean and I were there already. Igor let him know that we were at his place and that Patrick was the one who dropped us off there. Paskier told him he was on his way to meet with us as he had just gotten off work. I asked Igor what he thought about life on campus at Grayson County College. He first asked which dormitory I was going to stay in. I told him that certainly Mrs. Pearce was going to find a place for me in the Jensen dorm. Igor smiled after I said Jensen Dorm. Then I asked him what did he find funny about it. He did not seem to really like the idea of me staying at the Jensen Dorm. He told me that he had stayed in the Vikings Dorm located on the main campus while the Jensen Dorm was on the West side of the road leading to the campus. He added that his friends who lived at Jensen Dorm often had problems making it to the main campus because of the bus frequency and long waiting time. Sometimes, he added, they had to get up earlier than they could to catch the bus – even if class- schedules did not require for them to be on campus that early. This was a major issue at Jensen Dorm and he added that they always relied on the bus to participate in after class activities on campus. You could not stay at the library late because you needed to catch the last bus back to the dorm; otherwise, you would have to look for someone kind enough to give you a ride to the dorm. I told Igor that I was not told about all those issues and that I just thought the shuttle bus was effective enough to respond to the needs of all students who resided at Jensen. We both cooled off a little bit about that issue and Igor asked when I was going to enter the dorm. I told him the coming

126

weekend, as I needed to let my father know so he could send me money to pay for my tuition and living expenses on campus. Paskier finally arrived and we all stayed at Igor's apartment, chatting the rest of the time. Igor and Paskier painted a broad picture of Grayson County College, but also of the city of Sherman and how we needed to deal with people in the community. After about an hour, Paskier and Jean were ready to leave. I asked Jean what time he was going to be on campus the next day because we needed to meet with Mrs. Pearce again. He told me that he was going to be there after nine because he did not see any reason for him to be there earlier than that. He was right about that, so I let him know that I might be there a little earlier because Igor and I were going to catch up with Guy Patrick's schedule of classes to ride with him. They both left the room, and Igor and I remained in the living room before I told him that I felt exhausted and was going to take a nap. Igor was the kind of person whose nature you could not really determine. It was quite difficult to read what his thoughts were or how he reacted to situations. He was a quiet and calm guy who was passionate about video games. Igor could sit before his TV screen for hours and hours playing games while I would instead go enjoy a deep sleep. I looked at all those moments that I would go lie down and thought about the direction my life was taking and how everything that I was learning and experiencing was affecting my personality. I had not even been in Sherman, Texas for a month and already I was feeling the weight of a burden on my back. I recalled moments in high school with my friends of the Martin Luther King, Jr. English Club. I thought about the times we all dreamed about coming to America, meeting with Dr. King's family, and taking pictures of all the beautiful places in the country. But above all that, we all said to ourselves that we were going to attend the top universities of America and make ourselves known on campus there, just as we did at Gondjout High. I recalled one afternoon we sat under a huge tree that stood in the very center of Gondjout High School and we asked each other what university we were going to attend in America. My comrade Smith, who today

127

is pursuing his studies in South Africa, responded that he was going to attend Morehouse College in Atlanta, Georgia and he explained that he chose that school because Dr. King had a degree from there and he wanted to follow our mentor's steps. Gauthier chose NYU, which I had never heard about before he mentioned it. He said that he dreamed about living and studying in New York City and that if he could be in the States, which was where he was going to live and attend one of the city's top universities. Everyone else mentioned their choices of schools in America and when it came to me, I laughed and told my friends that I knew it may seem funny but a dream is a dream and that I dreamed about Harvard University in Boston, Massachusetts. When I said that Harvard was my choice, I remember Boris, another friend of mine from the club, looked at me stupefied. Then he asked if I was not looking too far or if I just wanted to tease them with that. I also laughed about it myself before I answered Boris, saying that nothing was wrong with dreaming and that was the whole point about dreaming. Everyone else joined us on that and we all laughed about it. However, before we moved onto another fellow to see what school he was going to choose, Smith put his arm over my shoulder and told me that he believed that I could attend Harvard if I really wanted to and that I just needed to find out what the requirements there were. I thanked him and then we moved to the other fellow. Our group at Gondjout High was composed of overly ambitious students, dedicated to studying not only English, but also to being the best in all the other subjects we had to learn about. We became more than just friends or teammates from the English Club. We were brothers and we began to look at Dr. King as our father and that we all needed to make him proud by doing well in school and raising high the name of our English Club in Gabon. The club was becoming a personal matter to me. I saw myself spending the night in my bedroom thinking about what was going to be the next activity in the club and how I was going to present it to my fellows and students who attended our classes. My friends at time, worried that I spent more time at the club than I did with my classes and being in my senior year and expected to pass the baccalaureate exam at the end of the year, I did not seem concerned with that. I assured my friends that I was doing all right in my classes and they did not have to worry about it because I always made sure that while in class, I grasped all that was being taught so that I did not have to worry about it after class was over and it really did work for me. At the end of the year, I passed my exam and stood among the top students of the year at Gondjout High School. The principal and all my instructors at Gondjout High were proud of me and congratulated my results, saying that they did not have any doubt about me passing the exam. I was a model student to talk about in their classes to inspire other students at Gondjout High. Often, when I recalled those moments, I wondered what my life would have been like if I had stayed in Gabon and studied at a local university. I had gained the renown of an intelligent and hard-working student at Gondjout High and I believed that because of that, I was forced to set higher expectations for my academic life. I said to myself that I needed to bring that renown back while studying at Grayson County College, and despite whatever issues I encountered, it surely should not stop me from growing my intellectual emulation and pursuit of my dream. As I lay down on his bed, thinking about my life and what I was going to do with it, Igor came in and asked if I wanted to go out and eat something for dinner. I told him I did not mind at all and if he were up to it, we could just go. So, we left the apartment and we did not need to call for a ride as Igor proposed to walk to a fast-food restaurant that was close to the other side of the complex. The idea was fine with me, and at least I could see the neighborhood and admire the nicely built homes that surrounded Fairview Apartments. We walked through a line of trees and I could see on the other side of the road Fairview Park. It reminded me of Mont Saint Vincent College in Riverdale, New York where I first went to ESL school. Squirrels climbing trees around the park made it look so peaceful and nice to just get there and have a fun time. After we passed a couple of houses, we arrived at the fast-food restaurant. A nice-looking blond-haired person walked toward us and after she greet us, asked if she could get the menu. Igor let her know that we did not need one because he already knew what we were going to have. Then he ordered fried chicken with French fries, assuring me that I was going to like it as well. I let Igor know that his order sounded delicious to me and that definitely I would go for it. It did not take too long before the lady called us and handed the order to Igor, who gave her the money, and we headed out. The weather was really nice outside that day and I truly did enjoy the walk back to the apartment. It was one more day over for me in Sherman, Texas. I would say that I did not really think about anything else that mattered to me other than getting to start classes and enter the dormitory. I enjoyed every single moment that I spent at Igor's and all the fun we had talking about the everyday life in Sherman – mostly in the African community, where Igor would share stories about our people who barely could behave differently than they did back home. He would for instance advise me about the high gossip going on in the African community about everyone's life, a gossip that we all labeled "congossa" to describe the dirty habit of talking about people's private lives behind their backs just for the sake of telling a story. "Congossa" was not something with which I was unfamiliar. In fact, one was a victim of "congossa" anywhere there was a group of Africans meeting on a regular basis. People would talk about one's dressing style; one's personal problems would be known to everybody; and things were shared that would upset anyone who gave serious attention to his privacy. I told Igor that I was already aware of it before I got to Sherman because although in New York City, people rarely got together just to talk because of the busyness in the city, there still were people who sought an occasion to just talk about others in a quite unpleasant manner. However, we mostly laughed about it and as we went along enjoying a pizza or a movie that Igor rented, the two of us thought about the beginning of classes and how each of us was going to set up a working study schedule to tackle every class more efficiently. The day that followed that night I spent to Igor's; we shared a ride with Guy Patrick to Grayson. I met with Mrs. Pearce, not for a long time because she just needed to give me a document that allowed me to go to the Jensen dormitory and get the keys for my room. I had already sent an email to my father, informing him of the cost of my tuition including the dormitory. He was going to send me the money the next day so I could assure Mrs. Pearce that I was ready to get my room. After Mrs. Pearce issued the document to me so I could go to Jensen dormitory and meet with the dorm supervisor, I needed to find a ride to that location, but as I could not find anybody available to take me there at that time, I decided to go to the library and wait there. There were a couple of unoccupied seats at the library when I got there and so I sat on one of them. After about a couple of minutes, a white lady approached me and she seemed worried about something when she asked if she could sit by me. I let her know that I did not find any problem with that. She introduced herself and told me her name was Kathy. I told her in return that I was Frank and that she was the second Kathy I met since I arrived at Grayson. We both laughed about it before she asked who the first was. I told her my advisor's name was Kathy Pearce and now she was another Kathy. Then, she asked where I was from and I eventually explained to her about Gabon and how she could locate the country on a map. It seemed easy for her to figure it out. Then, I told her I was sitting there to find someone who could give me a ride to the Jensen dorm so I could get the room's key and introduce myself to the supervisor before getting my things from Igor's and moving in. She did not even let me finish with all that I was trying to tell her and proposed to drive me there. At first, I tried to refuse and thank her kindness, but she insisted and did not want me to argue her offer, so I agreed and we both headed out of the library in direction of the parking lot where her car was parked. One more time I said to myself that I had a God who never left me alone and always proved his presence around me. Kathy and I drove to the Jensen dorm and as we drove, I noticed that the road to the dorm was a pretty empty one; I mean, there was nothing around except for dried trees and old-fashioned abandoned houses that gave the impression that we were heading to a nowhere location. I asked Kathy if she had resided in the dorm before. She told me she had never lived in a dormitory, but she knew a couple of friends who resided there and therefore could give them a ride occasionally if they could not make it on time for the shuttle bus. We finally got to the dorm. It was one huge, yellow-painted brick building with blue painted bands that surrounded the front wall. I got out of the car and Kathy told me she was going to wait for me until I was done with the supervisor. I walked to the door, a blue-painted two-sided door, and began to knock so someone could come and open it for me. There were a couple of students in the main room who I could see from the window outside. One of them walked to the door and opened it for me. I greeted and thanked him for coming out. Then I asked where I could meet with the supervisor. The guy asked if I meant someone named April, the lady in charge. I said yes and he walked me through the main room by another door that led to a laundry room and just after that room, he told me to wait in another room that opened on the other side of the hall. Then he rang the bell before a door that read Supervisor. It was April's room. She finally came out and as the guy let her know that there was a new student for her, she walked to me with a big smile, greeting me and asking for my name. I told her my name and she asked that I get myself a seat in the room while she brought the paperwork for me to fill out. There was an empty chair in the room with quite a long table, so I sat and waited for her to come back with a pile of documents. She let me know that I needed to take my time to fill them all out with as few errors as I could because she did not have other copies for me. I began reading the documents and filling out all that I needed to. It took me about fifteen minutes to get everything done. I was worried about Kathy, as I knew that she waited for me to just get the key and meet her in the car. After April checked all the documents I filled out, she asked when I was ready to move in. I told her I was ready to move in that very day. She gave

132

me the key to my room and proposed to walk me to the room, so I knew where it was by the time I came in later in the evening. We passed through the main room, which was like a lobby in a hotel, where residents could go to watch TV, play video games, and engage in other group activities. Then we walked through another of those blue doors and right behind it was my room. It was the very first door on the right side of the hall leading to the other rooms. She opened it and as we entered, I saw that there were already two small-sized beds and two study tables on each side of the beds; everyone had their own study table. There was already a TV and a microwave in the room, which to me seemed to already have someone living in there. April told me that my roommate was already there and that he was a nice guy so I did not have to worry about any problems with him. I thanked her for letting me know and as we walked out of the room, she put her arm around my neck and told me that if I had any problem at all, I should make sure to let her know. I told her I would, even though I did not think that was going to happen. I left the building and joined Kathy in her car. I apologized to her for having taken that much of her time, but she did not seem bothered at all. She even seemed surprised that I was back that quickly. I told her about the little tour April and I had in the room once I was done with the paperwork. She smiled and let me know that I did not have to hurry because of her; she did not expect me to be back that soon, anyway. As we drove back to the main campus, she asked what I was going to do next. I told her I did not have anything to do at school other than find someone to take me home to Fairview Apartment. Again, she surprised me by proposing to take me home, and as we drove, she told me she lived in the very same area and it was okay with her to take me home. I barely could say anything after that except to let her know that I did not know what to say to thank her enough for all that she did for me that day. She was so kind that I began to wonder what she really wanted from me and how she could be that kind to someone she just met for a couple of minutes. Well, I said to myself that certainly she was going to explain it to me whenever she wanted to do so and therefore, I could only thank her and appreciate her company. Kathy told me that she had three little girls and that she was a single parent and worked her way through school to get her degree at Grayson and continue to a four-year institution for a degree in Business Administration. She told me she had always been fascinated with Africa in general and that she hoped she one day could make it there for a visit. I told her it would be a pleasant experience for her and that if she could make it, her perception of life in general was going to change. We both agreed on that and the drive was not even long enough before we reached Fairview Apartments and she dropped me right at the main entrance before asking that I call her whenever I was ready to go to the dorm. She was going to take me back there the same night if I wanted. She had me write her phone number and promise that I call her later that evening. I left and as she drove away, I stopped and looked up to heaven, thanking God for what he was doing for me. Once in the apartment, I found Igor and other guys I had not met before that day. They were playing video games and I could tell by how noisy the room was that they all were as into video games as Igor was and so I headed to the room to gather all my belongings so I would be ready by the time I called Kathy. Igor joined me in the room after a couple of minutes as I had not joined them after I got there. I told him I was moving to the dorm that night and that I had met with a lady I had befriended and she proposed to take me to the dorm. When I told Igor about Kathy, he looked at me with an amazed look as if he could not believe what I had just told him. Then, he asked again about Kathy, this time, praising me for being one fast man who did not wait too long to get himself a girl. I tried to let him know that it was just a friendship type relation with Kathy, but he had already run out of the room and filled the others in about it. I suddenly had all of them around me laughing and asking that I share the story with them. Although I insisted that there was nothing but simple friendship with the lady, the guys did not want to buy that from me. So, they decided to wait until she came to pick me up so they could see what she looked like and how I acted with her. I went to get myself a shower and change before calling Kathy. Igor ordered pizza, which he wondered if I was going to have time to share with them. I told him not to worry about me and that I would love to take one with me to the dorm since I was not sure when I would be going out once there. He agreed on that although with a mocking air. After I was done with my shower and ready to leave, I asked for Igor's mobile phone so I could call Kathy. He did not mind that I use his phone, especially since they all were excited to see Kathy coming for me. She told me she was on her way after I hung up, and I let her know I was already ready. It did not take long for her to arrive. She did not stay far from the area since she had made it that fast. She did not have to get out of her car since I saw her coming. I just walked out with my bags and joined her, in the curious gaze of my friends whom I could see from the side window of the apartment. I bet they hoped to see me doing something that would prove them right about what they already had in their minds. But I decided to take it very professionally and greeted Kathy in a very friendly manner. We left the complex and as we drove away, she asked how I was feeling about leaving my friends. I told her that it really was not a big deal to me because eventually I was going to meet with them on campus as they all attended Grayson. When we arrived at Jensen, Kathy proposed to help me carry my stuff to my room and I agreed to that. We both made it to the room and as I located an empty spot in my closet, I put all my bags in there with the intention in mind to pull my clothes out and arrange them on the shelves after Kathy was gone. We both sat on my little bed and again I thanked her for all that she had done for me. For a moment, Kathy did not say a word, but looked around the room, then asked if I had shared a room with a foreigner before. I told her that when I was in high school in Gabon, I resided in a dormitory and shared a room with another student, so it really was not going to be an issue at all to me if my roommate and I showed respect to one another's principles. She laughed after I said that, and even though I wanted to know what was funny about it, I did not ask her to tell me. Then she stood up and told me she was ready to leave, as she had to go pick up her daughters from the daycare. I proposed to walk her to her car, but she did not agree with that; instead, she asked that I make sure to make myself at home in my new room and certainly we would meet on campus the next day. I did not want to insist after she refused that I walk her to her car so I gave her a hug and we both said goodnight to one another. My first night at the dorm was not as fun as I thought it was going to be. After I ordered my closet and made sure everything was where it was supposed to be in the room, I decided to go to the lobby, as there was nothing else to do in my room but sleep and I was not wanting to sleep yet. In the lobby, I met with other white students; they knew each other for a long time as they all talked about moments of fun they shared at Grayson. One of them seemed very funny and easy to approach. His name was Jonathan, a big white boy in his twenties with a voice not matching his age. He was a theatre major as the majority of his friends at the dorm. He walked toward me and introduced himself, then, asked where I was from. I told him about Gabon and Africa in general. Unlike many whom I had talked about it with before, Jonathan seemed to know much about Gabon and as we went along, talking about my country, he mentioned having met with another guy from Gabon in the dorm and that he also was a pretty cool guy and had just arrived from a school of language in Louisiana. I asked if he had seen him around that night, as I really wanted to meet with him as well. As Jonathan tried to think about it, I asked if he knew the guy's room number so I could look for him there. He gave me the room number, and as I walked there, trying to locate it, I found out that it was not too far at all from my room. I knocked about twice before someone answered and opened the door. I greeted the guy in French, as I knew that it was him for a reason. He answered in French as well, and as I introduced myself to him, I told him I was also from Gabon and that I thought I was the only African at Jensen, until Jonathan talked to me about him. We both laughed about it and he invited me in to have a seat so we could talk some more. It came to be as we kept talking that, Beranger, which was his name, was a Fang native; in other words, we shared the same native language. This was going to bond us even more, I told him, and the conversation from that moment switched from French to Fang. It felt so good to be with someone that close in the Jensen dorm. Beranger and I were not only the sole Gabonese students there, but also the sole African students among all others who attended Grayson County College. One could then understand how important it was going to be for the two of us to get to know each other better. Beranger had just transferred from an ESL school he was enrolled in at Louisiana Tech where he spent about a month attending English classes, the same as I did in Riverdale, New York. He talked to me about his sojourn there, especially how hard it was to get around the city, as it was quite impossible to go anywhere without having to get a ride. He told me about a night he and other students there had to walk through the Interstate to get to a convenience store so they could get something to eat as the university's cafeteria did not serve meals on weekends for them. Then he asked about my time in New York City, and before I even could begin saying anything, he asked how someone could leave New York City for Sherman, Texas. It sounded very funny to me so I laughed for a couple of minutes before I am assuring him that I did have an enjoyable time at my ESL school in Riverdale. I talked to him about the visit to the Bronx Zoo and the cool instructors at ESL. Then, I talked to him about life in general in the city of New York and its surroundings. However, I made sure Beranger understood that to me, all that was a myth that covered a quite bitter reality of life in New York and I would even say great cities in the world. I told him about my education and how continuing to live in New York City at that moment was going to jeopardize my academic pursuit. As I could see how hard it was getting for Beranger to follow my logic on that, I began to tell him about the pressure of jobs and the activities one could be attracted to while living in New York and as I managed to narrow the details to him, my friend began to agree with my decision and accept the ethics in that decision. Then he asked what I was going to major in at Grayson. I told him Political Science was my major and I hoped to go to law school after my bachelor's degree. Beranger joked after I told him about my major and with a very cool humor, asked if I was going to be the next ambassador of Gabon to the States. We both laughed about it but I added that it was a possibility. He was going to major in Business Administration but wanted to focus on finance once he went for his bachelors at a four-year college. Beranger was not the only one of some of the African fellows I had met in Sherman wanting to go for Business Administration at Grayson and then continue with finance at a four-year institution. As the conversation lasted hours, BJ and I almost forgot that we had class the next day and therefore needed to sleep. I said goodnight to my friend, now my brother, and we promised to continue our talks the next day. When I returned to my room, my roommate was there already. He was a big guy wearing reading glasses and a black T-shirt that almost reached his knees, covering his short-legged jean pant. "Hello," he said to me and I responded the same way. I do not remember what he said his real name was, but he insisted that I call him Messo as everyone else called him. I told him I did not really mind and that he could call me Frank. My roommate and I spent the rest of that night getting to know each other and talking about our academic pursuits. Messo was a theater major and hoped to get his associate degree at Grayson County College before going to a four-year institution on the East coast. He came from a small neighboring town, and because of the need for transportation, his family had arranged for him to live on campus during the semester and return home when classes were over. However, he also would get to go spend time with his family on weekends whenever he felt like it. I told him that although I had met good friends, mostly guys from my country, I did not have a close relative in Sherman, so I did not worry too much about off-campus visits on weekends like he would. We finally wished goodnight to one another, and as the next day was going to be a busy one, I let myself be taken away into the depths of a long sleeping.

The next day, as I got up early, my roommate was still sleeping and I first did not know if I had to wake him up or respect his sleeping. I headed to the bathroom and got into the shower. As the hot water rushed over my body, I began to recall those moments I spent in the dormitory at Gondjout High when all the guys would rush to be the first to get in the shower and enjoy the hot water, which would last only few minutes before switching to cold water, which no one wanted to feel on his body. It was funny to see guys jumping and screaming all around the bathroom, as they could not stand the freezing water. While standing there and feeling the hot water all over me, I felt like I was going asleep for a moment while on my feet. I brought myself back to the room and finished taking my shower. On my way out, I crossed paths with other guys who were exiting their rooms in direction to the shower. We said "Hi" and "Hello" to each other, and I got back into my room. Messo still was sleeping. I got dressed myself and while I was gathering my school documents, I decided to wake him up. I had just to reach his arm and softly shake him. Messo brusquely woke up, and looking all around me, asked what time it was. I told him it was almost fifteen minutes to eight o'clock. I did not even have to finish saying o'clock before Messo jumped from his bed, grabbed his towel, and exited the room in a rush I had not seen for a long time. The reaction was so fast that in the minute that followed, I began to laugh as loud as I could. The whole picture of the scene came back to me as a theatrical scene. As I recalled that Messo was a theatre major, I said to myself that he was going to do well in there. Minutes later, he came back to the room. As he walked to his closet, I asked what happened to him that he slept that long and was not being able to get up for class. He looked at me for a moment without a word and then he began to laugh about the whole scene. Then he told me he had always had a sleeping issue and that he would really appreciate it if I woke him up when I got up. I agreed and told him that I had thought about doing so when I got up, but I hesitated because I did not want to trouble his sleep. As we both finished getting ready, we left the room and walked out to the bus stop. Beranger was already standing out there by the time Messo and I arrived. I introduced the two of them and the three of us sat on the top of a bench by the bus's stop sign. As we waited for the bus to arrive, other students residing at Jensen began to one-by-one walk to the parking lot, each of them starting their cars, ready to head to the main campus. While looking at them, I began to think about what such a picture really betrayed. I suddenly recalled those college student series I used to watch while in Gabon. I thought about those movies depicting, the realities of American college life, where all students were independent and lived their lives just as they understood them. Here I was living the true American life. I saw students of a younger age, driving SUVs and vehicles of high standard while still in college. I looked at Beranger, and as our eyes crossed, he nodded his head, agreeing with me that now we were in the States. Soon, our bus arrived, and as we got in, both Beranger and I smiled, expressing our appreciation. Messo did not say anything at all, instead looking at Beranger and me, trying to figure out what we were smiling about. When we arrived at the main campus, I headed to Mrs. Pearce's office because I needed to get my class schedule from her before I could look for my classroom. Her office was not busy at all when I got there, so it did not take long for her to give me the schedule and for me to head out. My first class that day was an English course taught by a lady named Virginia Thompson. After I located the classroom, I made sure that I was not disturbing class as I managed to find a seat. The instructor asked that I introduce myself to the class. I stood up from where I found a seat at the very back of the class and said my name and where I came from. The class was an advanced level of basic English grammar and writing processes. I did enjoy my English class with Mrs. Thompson, and I could see that the fact that I was the sole African student in the class made it even more interesting because we could argue about subjects from different perspectives, and an

African student with English as a second language was one quite considerable. The rest of the day, I had to attend a mathematics class that introduced me to pre-algebra notions that would enable me to pass the math session of the Compass test. I had begun my first experience in a typical American college that year, and I could feel the motivation within me. I could see myself studying hard and being amongst the best students in all my classes. Sometimes, as I sat in a classroom before a class began and read my notes, I recalled my New York experience and realized how much time I had missed. I looked at my classmates, as everyone had their eyes focused on their notes or on a computer laptop, revising or doing research for a precedent class or the one that followed. I felt good sitting there in a classroom. This is where I was meant to be when I left home. This is where I told my father I was going and now that I could feel the joy and determination of learning, I promised myself I would succeed and make my way to the top universities of America. That same semester, I also registered for a speech class that was taught by a well-renowned instructor named Mr. Joe Hicks. The man was in his sixties and one could tell that he had experience in the teaching of his subject. I was referred to his class by another student from Gabon, whom I had met through Paskier. His name was Nze Akoue Axel. He had attended Grayson County College for two consecutive semesters and thanks to Mr. Joe Hicks and his connections, Axel was able to transfer to Austin College, the only four-year college with a strong accreditation in Sherman. I did not hear of many other fellow African students who attended Austin College, and I would say that this was an issue because of the high cost of tuition. Mr. Joe Hicks had had Axel in his speech class and from what I had heard from those who knew him before I did, was that he was so good at public speaking and behavior that he caught Mr. Joe Hicks's personal attention to the point he began to love him just like his own son. When I saw Mr. Joe Hicks the first day of class, I almost felt like I knew the man from before and therefore was excited to introduce myself to him and get started with the class assignments so I could follow Axel's path and make a good impression – not only to my instructor, but also to my fellow students. I remembered nights when I found myself in my room, standing before the mirror fixed to the closet door, interviewing myself about how far I wanted to go with my education in the United States of America. I would manage to sound as serious as I could and let myself know that my goal was to go to Harvard University and complete a Ph.D. from there. Furthermore, I became so enthusiastic about studying that I even began writing "Dr" before stating my name just to project myself in the person of a Ph.D. holder. I can still remember the day I paid tribute to Dr. Martin Luther King, Jr. during my speech class. Mr. Joe Hicks had asked that everyone work on a tribute speech to a person we considered a role model. I could not think of anyone else but Dr. King who was a role model not only to me but also to Americans and people around the world. My classmates did not seem to be taking their appearance before pupils too seriously. They dressed casually, even after Mr. Joe Hicks required that everyone be dressed professionally for their presentation. The day of my presentation, I arrived in class suited with a tie that fitted my suit, making me stand more as an instructor than a student. My classmates could not keep their eyes off me, wondering what I was thinking, dressing like that. I knew what I was doing and knowing that I had everybody's attention smoothed my presentation. Moreover, I could make Mr. Joe Hicks smile, which was a first in that class. When I handed my paper over to him, he complimented me for the suit I wore. Then I stood before my classmates and suggested that the light be dimed during the speech, because I needed to use the projector; I had included a slide of pictures and images of Dr. King that I wanted to show to the class. I began by introducing myself, saying my name, and thanking the whole class for their attention; Then, I began to talk about the biography of Dr. King, from his academic successes to his life in the ministry as a co-pastor with his father at Ebenezer Baptist church in Atlanta, Georgia to his determination to actively participate in the Civil Rights

142

movement that would change the position of African-Americans in the United States of America. As I moved from one aspect of the man's life to another, I followed the shift with pictures and images that related to the aspect I was bringing up, and I could feel everyone's deep attention and admiration of Dr. Martin Luther King, Jr. It was as if none of them had heard about him before and that I was the first to call to their attention who Dr. Martin Luther King, Jr. was and why he should be a role model to all of us regardless of where we came from. I finally mentioned my personal interest in his character, and how, as a former member of the MLK English Club in Gabon, I had dedicated much of my time to reading about Dr. King and his bond to the principles of non-violence in solving conflicts. I ended the speech by inviting everyone to read about the man and his principles when they left class so they could feel why I believed he should be a role model to them as well. I had not finished saying thank you to the class when everyone stood up and rained applauses that led me to my seat. The lights were turned on, and as I walked to my place, my eyes staring at Mr. Joe Hicks, I said to myself that I did possess the public speaking skill within me and I was going to improve it. Mr. Joe Hicks stood up from where he sat and as he walked to the pupil in front of the class, he asked that I joined him there. First, I thought he was just going to make his comment as he did for everyone else, even though he had never asked for anyone to join him in front of the whole class. Then, when I got there by his side, he began speaking with the class and told them that he had been teaching public speaking in colleges for fourteen years and at this class level, he never had had a student give such a brilliant presentation as I had. He turned to me and personally thanked me for my presentation. I did not know what to say, as the whole thing was more than I had expected, so I thanked him as well for sharing his experience with us and thereby inspiring me to do well. As I returned to my seat, all my classmates applauded and again, I felt so overwhelmed that I almost shed tears of joy. I was proud of myself and happy about the impression I had made on my instructor and on my fellow classmates. After my speech class, as I walked out of the room, Mr. Joe Hicks asked that I meet with him in his office because he needed to talk to me personally. We both walked to his office when everyone else had left the classroom; then, he asked me about my academic goals and how I intended to go for them. I told Mr. Joe Hicks that I sought a bachelor's degree in political science and international Relations after I was done at Grayson County College, and that my dream was to attend Harvard University. Mr. Joe Hicks stared at me with a profoundly serious expression as I detailed my academic goals and plans. Then, after I was done speaking, he first smiled and told me that he believed that I could make it to Harvard or any other school that I desired to attend because he felt the vibe and motivation within me and that was a major asset for an excellent student. Finally, he told me that if there was something that I needed from him to help me move forward with my education, I should not hesitate to contact him. I told him that I deeply appreciated his concern and that surely, I would let him know of anything he might be able to help me with. We shook hands and I walked out of the office. "What a day!" I said to myself. I surely was ready when leaving the dorm to make a good presentation and get a good grade but was not prepared at all for all that came through that day. It was just interesting to see how sometimes we set ourselves at a certain level, passionately believing that was the only place we could stand and later finding out that we could go higher than that initial level at which we positioned ourselves. Now, more than ever, my speech class had confirmed to me that I really could make it to Harvard. It felt like a deep burn within me, and only studying more could relieve the pain. I promised myself that nothing else was going to be a major concern for me other than my studies and my academic progress. I did not know yet what life was going to bring and the irony about all that was that I was quite aware of the many changes that were going to come after the semester was over and I needed to look for a job and a place off campus, but still, I kept strongly believing that everything was just about my studies and nothing was going to block me from succeeding. Days and months had passed after my father sent me money to pay for my tuition and living expenses at the dorm that allowed me to get meals every day from Monday to Friday; because the plan I paid for did not include weekend meals, I would have to find ways to provide for my own food on Saturdays and Sundays. My friend Beranger also did not pay for a weekend meals plan, so we both stayed at the dorm when other dorm residents went to the cafeteria to have their breakfast in the morning, lunch later at noon, and dinner to close the day. It was interesting how Beranger and I managed to provide for our meals. He purchased a microwave to keep in his room and my roommate already had one in our room, which he gave me permission to use anytime I needed to. So, Beranger, who later I called BG, and I would get a ride from other residents whom we had really befriended and go to Wal-Mart or other grocery stores where we would get food and drinks that mostly needed just to be heated in the microwave and fill our refrigerators as weekend provisions. Sometimes, I remember Jonathan, one the guy's BG and I spent more time with and shared jokes about Africa and life in Sherman. He would come knock on our doors on Saturday or Sunday mornings while we would still be sleeping and propose to give us a ride to the city so we could discover what Sherman had to offer to us. He was a very opened-minded and amusing guy whom everybody at Jensen liked. He owned a red-colored Jeep Cherokee, which often reminded me of an uncle back home who had the exact same car. It was just so amazing to me how kids in America could own cars like those while back home, one needed to have a particularly good job or do some sort of business to own a personal vehicle. Moreover, I could not stop thinking about learning how to drive. The more I looked at those kids start their cars and drive as fast as they could with such confidence I saw only actors in James Bond movies, the more I said to myself that I needed to learn how to drive. One night, I recall, as Beranger and I walked outside the building, looking at the stars and the illuminant moon while talking

145

about our hopes and dreams for successful tomorrows, Jonathan drove by and stopped between the two of us. Then he asked if any of us knew how to drive. Beranger told him he could drive but had not tried an automatic car because back home, he only drove a stick. Then, I told him I had never held the wheel by myself, so I did not know how to drive at all but would surely love to learn how. Jonathan could not believe that from me and I kept telling him that it was the truth. Finally, he stepped out of his car and asked who wanted to get in first. I told BG to go first because I wanted to see how he did it, as he already had an experience on the wheel. He voluntarily stepped in the car as Jonathan got in the passenger side, and as my friend started the engine, I looked at him proudly and told him to go easy on his gas. As I stayed aside, at a distance away from the car, Beranger began to step on the gas and drive. He was good and I could only admire him as he drove away from the building and went all the way down by a golf course, which extended behind Jensen dorm. I could not see them anymore as they kept going farther and farther. Certainly, my friend was enjoying the ride, especially as he was the one giving it. After a couple of minutes, I could see them again, driving back towards where I stood waiting for them. As they reached the parking lot, Beranger managed to park the car between the yellow lines as all other cars were parked, but he barely made it straight in there, as his back tires remained out of the lines. My friend made it, and to me, he passed the test already. They both stepped out and Jonathan walked toward me, laughing and applauding BG, who asked how I thought he did. I proudly told him that he did so well he just needed to go get his driver's license the very next day. The three of us laughed about it and Jonathan opened the driver's door, pointing at me as to say, "Frank, it is your turn."

I cannot very well describe the feeling that got into me at that instant, but I knew that I was not as excited as I was before Jonathan asked that I take the wheel. I decided nevertheless to give it a shot and experience what it felt like to drive. As I started the engine,

Jonathan, I guess, understood that I was not confident enough. He talked to me and let me know that I did not have to worry about anything because he was on my side and was going to guide me all the way. I felt better after Jonathan talked to me and so I put my foot on the gas and we were gone. I did not truly realize that I was driving the car until we had completely left Jensen and gotten far across the golf course where Beranger drove earlier. Jonathan could not stop laughing and telling me that I was driving well and that he did not understand why I felt so uncomfortable before that. I was too cautious at the wheel so I could not even share the laugh with Jonathan as we went along the golf course. Then we reached a point where I needed to back up and head back to Jensen. Jonathan asked that I slow down and switch my foot to the brake so I could put the car on reverse and turn around. The experience of reversing was not easy for me, but I made it with Jonathan's help and good instructions. On my way back to Jensen, I began to feel increasingly comfortable with the idea that I was the one in control of the wheel. Jonathan continued to talk to me and I would say that it did help reduce my stress as I drove the car to the parking lot at Jensen. Beranger was waiting for us on the other side of the parking lot and I could see him pointing his thumb up to tell me that I was doing well at the wheel. Finally, I parked the vehicle and as soon as I turned off the engine, I let out a loud breath, thanking Jonathan for his kindness. Jonathan really was a cool guy; he took it very naturally to let Beranger and I drive his car. After that first driving experience, I decided to go apply for my driver's license, as I was ready to learn the driving code and pass the test, which I did in the weeks that followed. Having a driver's license to me was another big step I had made while in Texas. I was almost convinced that things were going to work for the good in Sherman and I would not have to worry about anything but doing well in school. As the semester ended, Mrs. Pearce asked that I meet with her in her office after I was done with my classes. Once I got there, she handed a document to me, which she asked that I fill out my personal information on and take it to the

Social Security office in Sherman. The document was a letter she was writing to the SSA, explaining that I was eligible to apply for a Social Security Number. I did not know what this was for and so she told me that it would help me apply for an apartment off campus when the semester was over; plus, I could get a job on campus with it. After I left Mrs. Pearce's office, I walked to the cafeteria and could not stop thinking about how quickly things were working for me in Sherman. I even began to regret all the time I spent in New York, saying to myself that if I had moved to Sherman after my ESL School in Riverdale, I would have progressed with my studies, and settled better. But I thanked God and concluded that surely my stay in New York was valuable and, I should appreciate it as such. As I became more familiar with the city of Sherman, and as the semester ended, I also began to think about what the next step was going to be when the dorm closes. Eventually, I knew that I was going to have to look for a place to stay off campus during the period the campus was going to be closed, but I could not decide where and with whom I would stay. One night, as Beranger and I watched a movie in the lobby, I brought the subject up to my friend and asked him if he had already thought about a place to stay after school was over. He also did not know where to go and with whom to stay. Without hesitating, I then suggested to him that we should look for an apartment to rent and be roommates. The idea did not seem to bother Beranger at all; on the contrary, he even suggested that we begin to prospect different apartment complexes so that we would be better informed before deciding on one place. I felt profoundly relieved from a psychological burden after Beranger agreed to look for a place with me and become my roommate. I needed though to inform my father about it so he would have enough time to save money for the rental fees by the time Beranger and I moved in. It had been quite a time since I had phoned him or any of my relatives back home. I had been so caught up with the semester and trying to get accustomed to my new location that I could not manage free time to check on my family. On the other hand, I did not worry too much about it because

I knew that if anything had happened, my father would have emailed me or found a means to get a hold of me. His silence then meant no news to me. We had reached the first week of May, and as finals approached, I felt the need to talk to my father. When his phone began to ring – after I had purchased a calling card from a convenience store, as that was where most Africans and even other foreign students got them – I began to think about what his questions were going to be and how I should address them to give satisfying answers. He finally responded, and as we went along with the conversation, he asked how school was going and how I felt about Sherman, Texas. I assured him that Sherman was a nice small town, especially for students, as it did not have all the movement and distracting activities one encountered in New York City. I knew that my father was going to like that part because he had always believed that a good student needed to live in a place with no distraction of any sort. I personally agreed with him about that, and Sherman somehow corresponded to that typical place my father talked about. Then we talked about my classes and my instructors and how good of a student I was being in all my classes. After that, I informed my father of the need for me to rent an apartment by the end of the semester, as I would not be able to stay on campus anymore. He asked if I had already found an apartment and with whom I was going to stay. I told him about Beranger and let him know that we were going to share the bills, but I needed to have money for the first month of the rent. My father agreed to help me with that. I just needed to give him a call whenever Beranger and I had everything set up. Before we said good-bye to each other, I asked my father if he had heard anything new about my scholarship. The situation was still hard on him, as he retained his breath for a minute and told me that he had been to the office where scholarship issues were dealt with and that no one gave him any attention and he did not believe they were going to grant me that scholarship at all. After I heard my father's response, I felt a little discouraged for a moment, and he could feel it. So, he asked that I always remember that God would never let me down, and that he always kept his promises; therefore, I should not let myself down because of that scholarship issue. If God had allowed me to come to the States, He also was going to provide for me to reach my goals without that scholarship. My father always had the words to bring me up and help me stand stronger. I asked that he greet the entire family on my behalf and that he tells my twin sister that I was going to call her later, and then we ended our communication.

My father has always been a spiritual mentor to me and being away from him was allowing me truly to experience our bond. There were days when I wanted to give up and return home to my father's side. But then I reminded myself that he would not want it to be like so. My father always looked up to me with grand expectations, though, at times I questioned the burden of those expectations, believing myself to be too young to have to live up to his expectations. Today, I understand that the sense of responsibility has nothing to do with a man's age. It is more about one's ability to maintain a stronger sense of value and purpose in the face of life's challenges. Being on point to renting my own apartment forced me to realize that I no longer was going to be my father's boy, but rather, a man whom my family could count on. Surely, in New York I already had experienced living on my own, but this time was different. There were going to be far more responsibilities, along with remaining in school to maintain my legal status in the United States. The urgency of the moment was for me to find a job and rely less on my father's financial assistance for my basic needs. My stay in Texas marked the onset of a new chapter in the story of my life as an international student, but as a man ready to awaken my inner-sleeping giant.

"Awakening the Sleeping Giant"

School was over, and Beranger and I had already moved into our new apartment at Hilltop Village. The apartment complex was located right on the side of Texoma Parkway, which also led to Denison, Texas, the nearest neighboring town. I found it quite difficult to identify the border lines between Sherman and Denison, but it was a matter of time before it all became clear. There were several other international students, especially Africans, and a respectable number of Gabonese students residing at Hilltop Village apartments. Beranger and I thought that it was a clever idea to be closer to everyone else, especially because we did not have a vehicle yet and therefore had to rely on other friends to give us a ride occasionally as the need would present itself. The apartment was a two bedroom with a master bedroom, which I had chosen to occupy since my friend didn't object . The kitchen was spacious with a fridge, an oven, and a dishwasher, making everything appear so nice for us. I personally liked everything about that apartment. Beranger and I were going to share all the charges and agreed to sometimes help one another whenever unexpected hardships made either of us unable to meet his monthly obligations. We were brothers and it was the least we could do to support one another. As we moved in, we also began to look for jobs in the surrounding areas, believing that it would be easier for us to find a job closer to the complex so we did not have to worry about transportation to get to work. Fortunately for the two of us, about two weeks from the time we moved in and began filing applications in restaurants and warehouses close to Hilltop, we both received a phone call from a restaurant named Red Lobster; it was located just on the other side of the Texoma Parkway, making it the closest job from home. Beranger and I only had to cross the road to be at work. We did not need to even think about asking for a ride. We had both applied for dishwasher positions, and they hired the two of us the very same day. This was more than a strike of luck; it was a sign from my God that He would always provide the best for me. I had prayed for Him to allow Beranger and I to get a job because not only did I need to have one to be able to pay for the rent and other living expenses, but also because I wanted to help my father by being able to save enough money to pay for my tuition by myself the next semester. Being able to do so would allow my father to focus more on my siblings back home. I sometimes felt bad whenever I had to call my father and ask for money because I knew that although he would do all he could to send me money, he also was going to feel bad for my brothers and sisters who would have to do with what he had left after sending the money to me. I challenged myself to be able to take care of myself from then on and that I would need my father's help only when I had no other options left to solve whatever financial problem I faced. After Red Lobster hired us, Beranger and I barely saw one another, even while living in the same apartment. Our working schedules were such that he had to work when I did not and I had to work when he was home. Plus, both of us had decided to register for summer classes, which did not make things any easier. I attended my summer class in the day, while Beranger had his classes in the evening. We always managed to arrange a ride to school and from school with friends who had similar schedules and I would say that for a while, things worked fine, until the day Beranger and I were forced to quit our jobs at Red Lobster, a month before the beginning of the next semester. Things could not get any worse; we had to leave Red Lobster because of a succession of issues that betrayed the true nature of one of the main supervisor's feelings toward Beranger and me. In fact, without having to get into all the details of what caused us to leave Red Lobster, I would say, that I enjoyed and knew that Beranger, too liked the job we had and we could honestly not have asked for better at that time. From my experience at Nonis restaurant in New York, the assignments I was required to complete at Red

Lobster were a piece of cake and I was making sure that I always did extra tasks to show how much of a determined and hard-working person I was by nature and hoped that all my supervisors at Red Lobster would like that and treat my friend and me with the respect and consideration we deserved. Beranger and I ran the dishwasher like two unstoppable machines and made sure that plates and all that was given to us to clean were ready at the time they were needed. Sometimes, because we worked so quickly and did such an efficient job, we would go look around the kitchen, in search of anything to clean, staying busy during our entire shift, especially on days we were called to work together. I still recall one day that the store's chief manager, a New York born gentleman who moved to Texas for business, walked in the kitchen for inspection, and could not stop staring at Beranger and me as we ran the dish washer with amazing pleasure, not even noticing that he was staring at us. Then, he walked up to us and asked where we were from. We both at the same time answered that we were from Gabon in Africa. He had a smile on his face and we could see that the man was impressed with our work ethic. He introduced himself and told us he was the chief manager and that he often came to pay unannounced visits in the restaurant to see how everyone was doing. Then, he added that he was happy to have the two of us at Red Lobster. Beranger and I told him we, too were happy to work at Red Lobster, and then he left and wished us a good day. Red Lobster was always busy. One could not really say that we had slow hours. From the time the restaurant opened, people would begin to come, and it would be like that the entire day. There were days Beranger and I worked the same schedule and I would say that we did have fun, but we really did have dishes to wash. While working at Red Lobster, I began to see how valuable my experience at Nonis Restaurant in New York City was. I operated the dishwasher at a speed that even Beranger wondered where I had learned to operate that machine with such ease. We would laugh about it, and I sometimes would talk to him about my experience at Nonis Restaurant. Everyone in the kitchen enjoyed our company as we always brought the fun while working, until the day one of the supervisors was not having a good day and took it out on Beranger and me. I still remember that evening. We did not stop washing dishes from the time we both clocked in to later in the evening, and everyone else had already left the restaurant, as we had passed the closing hours. The lady told us that we could not leave at all if all the dishes were not cleaned and the entire kitchen swept and mopped out. Beranger and I were exhausted and we tried to let the lady know that we really were exhausted and that she needed to let us go, but she did not seem to mind us at all. So, we worked ourselves hard to finish washing the dishes, and swept and mopped the entire kitchen floor. We thought that after we had that done, the supervisor would allow us to leave, especially since we had to open the restaurant the next morning. Unfortunately for us, by the time we walked to the lady to let her know that we were done, she did not seem any satisfied, instead walking us to another room which she asked that we sweep and mop. We began to really feel like she was taking her bad mood out on us and I guess, because of the strong esteem and respect Beranger and I shared for our personality, we had to let her know that we could not do what she was asking. Not only had we passed the normal working hours, but she was not being nice to us at all, instead, bossing us around the kitchen, claiming that we could not go home until everything appeared spotless to her appreciation. As Beranger and I stood before her, trying to bring her to good sense with us, she walked to her office and reminded us that we needed to obey her orders and get back to working. As she walked back to her office, the look on my friend's face said it all, we could no longer take it, so we walked ourselves out and went home. I guess someone would say that we should not have left that night, but I could see and feel the anger in Beranger's eyes, and even though I could have managed it otherwise, I knew that Beranger had reached his limits of tolerance and I shared his feelings that night. I just could not see myself working there again, without Beranger around in the kitchen, I knew that after that night, things were not going to be the same

154

again. I honestly could not come to understand what caused that supervisor to be so rude to us that night, but I am quite sure that we could not face her another day after the way she treated us.

The next day, as we did not show up to work, Red Lobster called, and it was the general manager himself who asked that we go meet him and discuss what happened because he knew that Beranger and I performed an excellent job and were respectful guys. He sounded very bothered by the fact that we did not make it to work. He insisted that we call him back whenever we heard his message. I asked Beranger what he thought about the manager's call and if we should go meet him or not. He told me that it did not really matter to him because under no circumstance was, he going to work to Red Lobster again and have to respond to that lady as supervisor. I agreed with him about that and we both decided to just ignore the call and begin to think about finding another job somewhere else. After days passed, the manager at Red Lobster understood that we had decided to quit and so he did not call anymore.

Beranger and I kept looking for other jobs, and I would admit that it was not easy at all to find another job that fast in Sherman. I managed to have my part of rent paid for in advance with the little savings I had accumulated while working at Red Lobster. Soon, I began to realize that quitting the job at Red Lobster was not such a clever idea, especially living off campus; you could not really expect anybody to pay for your charges. I knew that I could not call my father all the time to ask for help to pay for rent and other monthly charges because he was going to provide for my tuition the next semester. I needed to find a job so badly that I began to walk in every single company or staffing service in Sherman with a "now hiring" sign. It reminded me of those days in New York when I first began looking for a job. The difference with this time was that in New York City, it was fun to just walk from one street to the other and pass through different avenues, while in Sherman people did not walk at all. Everyone had a car or some sort of transportation to move from one place to the other, and my walking by highways and mid-roads was a little abnormal. I can still see those cars driving by and asking if everything was all right with me as I kept walking and looking for hiring signs. In New York City, no one would stop when they saw you walking and that was because most people walked in New York City. Sometimes when it would get too hot, I would think about New York City and just hope Sherman was a little bit like there. The distances were long from one plaza to another. I did not have other options but kept looking for a job and hoped someone somewhere will offer to give me a ride back home by the time I was done looking. After weeks had passed and I still had not found a job, I began to stress out because I did not have any savings at all and the deadline for rent was quickly approaching. My friend Beranger had enrolled for the first summer classes, so he was pretty busy with his classes and did not seem worried about looking for another job at that time. As I realized that I was not going to be able to make rent that month, I decided to talk to Beranger and ask if he could help me out and I would pay him back by the time I get the job. I did not feel good about the idea of asking him to do that especially since we had just moved together. It did not seem fair to me because I knew that he too was on his parents' support and therefore the little money he had for certainly enough to help him with his charges too. But did I really have a choice? Sometimes in life there are situations in which you just must do what you have to do and set aside your ego. Beranger's response surprised me from within. He did not seem to be bothered at all by my asking that he pay my part of the rent for that month; instead he was glad to help me out and told me that he clearly understood that I was looking for a job and that if I had had one, I would not be asking such a favor from him. He added that he was sure that if he were to be in a same situation, he could count on me to help him. I assured him that I would not even think twice about giving him a hand if that were to happen. The day after I talked to him, I did not go out looking for jobs again. I decided to just stay home and read as I had not done so since the semester ended.

Working at Red Lobster did not leave me any time to sit and do my reading, as I often returned home exhausted and ready to just go to bed. I began reading all that I was taught during the semester, especially my public speaking courses with Mr. Hicks, which reminded me of all the presentations I had given in class. Mr. Joe Hicks told me that he believed that I could do great in public speaking and communication and that I needed to join debate teams to improve my skills. He told me he was going to search for schools with such programs and see how we could arrange for me to join. I also pulled my English coursework from the classes I took at ALCC in New York to those I had taken during the last semester. It felt good to read those courses again and remind myself of what my purpose really was. I needed to stay focused as I promised my father I would. Things were not easy for me at all, especially without a job in Sherman. I looked around Hilltop Village where most internationals resided. There were students from Gabon, others from Cameroon, Senegal, Mali, Pakistan, and Nepal also. I had never heard of that country until I moved to Sherman. They too went through the same process most students from Gabon at Grayson County College went through. I supposed that there was someone in Nepal who did the exact same job Mrs. Dahir did in Gabon. We all lived at Hilltop Village. It was funny to open your window and hear people speaking French or African dialects outside. It felt like home at times. We would visit each other at any given time just to have company when feeling lonely. We would gather at one's apartment to show our support and love in moments of pain or troubles. I still remember the day when one of the students, a girl from Gabon named Bricia Mayombo, received news from home that her father had passed away. She could not even go for reasons we did not know, even if we did not really ignore them. A message was sent to every one of us residing at Hilltop that we needed to meet and discuss how to show our love and support to our sister. Mathew and Guy Patrick were the ones who sent the message and coordinated the meeting. They had been in Sherman a couple of years before us so they were considered the senior brothers at Hilltop. We decided that everybody would contribute what money they were able to come up with and we could make out a check that would be handed to Bricia to help her pass through the painful moment she was facing. Money was not what Bricia really needed at that time, but we knew that by doing so, we were showing our support for her to know that she had people around who loved her and sympathized with her.

After everybody had put in his or her contribution, we all walked to Bricia's apartment. She was not expecting her apartment that day to be filled up with the entire student community of Hilltop. People knocked at her door the entire day, there were no more seats in the room, and we were sitting on the carpet while others preferred to just lean on the walls. The emotion was too strong for Bricia to bear. She would begin to cry and thank us all for being there for her. Her girlfriends would hold her, when her phone rang, and she had to talk to her family back home. After everybody had made it to Bricia's apartment, Guy Patrick demanded that we all stand for a minute of silence to honor Bricia's late father. He began to say a prayer as we all closed our eyes in respect of his prayer. Then, he walked to Bricia, holding her arm, and he asked that Mathew brings the check to her as he spoke to her.

"Bricia," he said, "We know what you are going through now, even though not all of us could personally relate to your pain. We would like you to remember that you have a family around here and that although we all come from different homes, we share the same experiences as we all left our families to come to the United States. We become family and today we are required by that love to come to you and show our support and care in this moment you need us the most. Here is a check from the little contributions made by your family at Hilltop Village. We know it is not really what you need the most now, but we also know that it is going to help you somehow. We want you to be strong and always remember that there are people around here who care about you.

As he handed the check to Bricia, her eyes could not stop shedding tears. Bricia did not know what to say, and we could all understand her. But after a moment, she stood up from where she sat on the carpet. "I just want to say thank you to all of you all. I do not really know what else to say right now, but I am relieved to know that I have people around here who care for me and could share my pain, especially now of my life where I am never going to see my beloved daddy."

It was difficult for her to end those words without succumbing to tears again. She could not hold it, but she continued. "I know that each of you have your personal issues as we all know how it is to live here as international students, but you all have chosen to set a time for me today. I want you all to know that I love you all too and I that I will never forget what you are doing today. Thank you again."

As she walked to her room to put her check away I presumed, everyone continued with their talking and conversations to warm up the place, and it lasted the whole night. We made jokes, to make her laugh a little and help relieve her pain. Friends talked about summer classes and the funny people they were meeting on campus. Others mentioned those everyday stories at Hilltop Village in which a neighbor would complain about the loud music in one's apartment as some apartments were already labeled "show rooms" because the tenants had parties going on all the time. The atmosphere around everyone was one of brotherhood and sisterhood. It was in fact true that as foreign students at Grayson County College residing in Sherman, Texas, we shared the same issues although we did not have the same difficulties solving these issues. My friend Guy Patrick often would remind me of this whenever we talked about our community at Hilltop. He would tell me that of the things he had learned since he came to the States; one was that, as true as it was that we all shared the F-1 visa status of foreign students in America, we did not have the same difficulties in maintaining that status when times got hard. What Guy meant was that as F-1 visa students, we

159

all had the obligation to remain in good academic status or else lose our Visa status and be subjected to deportation at any time possible. International students had to live every single day of their sojourn in the country with that stressful obligation. Guy told me about students he knew who because they could not afford to pay for their tuition anymore due to financial hardships in their home country, and by not allowing their families to take care of them, lost their student status and were sent back. One of them committed suicide months later after he was sent back to his country and could not even find a place to stay. I just could not imagine how painful and heartbreaking that could be where I to ever face such pressure. It was like shutting off someone's main dream and leaving them with no reason to hope for a better future. Guy and I ended the conversation by promising to always do everything possible to maintain our status and do well in school; we had the potential to do well. I personally could not imagine what it would be like if I lost my status and got sent home with nothing. I know that it would break my father's heart and leave me with no reason to stand before my people and hope to be taken seriously at all. Every single day, I had to remind myself that it was the entire name and hope of my father that I carried with me, and that if anything happened to me, it would either raise up or tarnish his person. I asked God in my daily prayers to help me maintain my status and bless me with opportunities to do well in all my classes so I could get scholarships and help pay for my tuition. There was a girl I was introduced to at Bricia's apartment; her name was Murielle, but for a reason everybody kept calling her GPA. I did not understand why they called her that. I asked Guy why she was called GPA and why she did not seem to be bothered by that. Guy explained to me that she did not do anything else in her life but study. She had managed to maintain as in all her classes, and every instructor at GCC knew about her. She was even awarded a scholarship at GCC that paid for her books and a part of her tuition. After Guy explained that to me, I decided to introduce myself to Murielle and befriend her. She was cool and an incredibly open person. She always smiled and at first sight, did not really give the impression of who she was. I asked her what she majored in at Grayson and what she wanted to do when she graduated from GCC. She told me she was majoring in General Studies and was planning to study International Relations when she left Grayson. She had just one semester left before she graduated. I asked where she thought of going after she was done with Grayson. She told me she had applied to the University of Arkansas in Fayetteville and she had already received positive news from the school. She surely was going to be offered a scholarship to continue her education there. I looked at Murielle as the perfect example of the kind of people I needed to hang out with. I could read the determination to succeed in her eyes as she talked to me about her academic goals. Moreover, I could see myself in her. It made me just want to leave the place and go read my books and study for the coming semester even though I did not know yet what classes I was going to take. The idea came to me though that I should ask Murielle what classes she recommended I take for the next semester. She had already taken most of the classes I was required to take at GCC before I could graduate.

"I think you could help me decide of some of the classes I could take next semester," I asked her.

"It is not a problem at all, Frank. You have to tell me what classes you have already taken so we could figure out what would be better for you to have next."

"I already took my Public Speaking class and two of the basics English classes I was required to take after I took the compass test. Now, I do not know what should come next."

"Oh! That is easy, Frank. I think that you should register for English 1301 and a history class, too. I can even recommend an instructor to you for your English class."

"I am fine with that, Murielle! Who would you recommend that I take for English 1301?"

"Well, I think you should have Mrs. Patterson. I had her for my English 1301 and 1302 classes. I have to warn you that few international students would take her."

"Why is that?"

"Well, Frank, it is said on campus that she keeps her students busy and that she really does not mind whether or not English is your first language. Plus, she loves poetry and there are few students who like poetry, not even American students. But I have enjoyed her classes, because she helped me become better in my writings and I just had to read to get my A grades."

"Hum! I now understand why everyone keeps calling you GPA! Well, I like to have instructors who have that kind of reputation on campus. I think I will register with that Mrs. Patterson."

"That is cool, Frank. Matter of fact, she is having English 1301 for the Summer 2, which is next month. I think you should take it, so that you could take English 1302 during the fall semester. I could talk to her and let her know that you are my brother and hope that she is not going to be too hard on you Frank!"

She laughed after she said that and I could only stare at her, trying to figure out what she really meant by that. Then, she said, "Well Frank, I know you are going to get an A with her and represent me valuably. I know that she might just make you work hard because of me, but I guess you would enjoy that, wouldn't you?"

"Sure, Murielle! I think because of you I am going to have to double my efforts with Mrs. Patterson. I am going to register for next month and just do it as you suggest. I would need your writings, though, just to have an idea of what I am going to be doing.

"No problem, my brother. I always keep my copies for all the classes I take and I would not mind lending them to you to study and do well with Mrs. Patterson."

"Thank you so much, Murielle! You really are a sister and I would let you know of how I would be doing when classes begin."

"Okay, Frank!" She replied before we walked back to Guy, whose facial expression betrayed his wondering mind.

It really was good to talk with Murielle. I felt like I had passed a job interview and that I was ready to start working. Murielle had boosted my spirit, making me excited hjabout taking that English 1301 class the next month. I explained to Guy that we just talked about school and how we sometimes could work together on courses.

"Yea, I did not think that the conversation could go off school stuff anyways, with the GPA," Guy said in a mocking tone.

"Well, my friend, I did not expect to go off that subject either, so I am not disappointed at all," I said.

We both laughed for a moment about it as people began to say good-bye to Bricia and remind her that she could call anytime she felt like it. Bricia was not crying anymore. I guess our presence and the fun some of us brought in her apartment calmed her a little and helped her set aside her pain. Then, Guy and I stood up and went to give her a hug, promising to come check on her whenever we had a chance. Guy suggested that she took a break or days off from work and just stay home for a moment. She told him she was going to talk to her supervisor the next day and hoped they allowed her to take days off. I told her she could call me anytime, as I was her closest neighbor in the complex. Her apartment was on the second floor of my building so we saw each other often, despite our schedules, which did not favor regular interaction between us. She thanked Guy and me for being there for her.

We left Bricia's apartment and I suggested that Guy stop by my apartment so we could share a drink and just continue our talking. He told me he had to work early the next day, as he was the one to open the convenience store where he worked. I told him that was fine with me and that we surely could do it other days. He walked to his car and I returned to my apartment. Beranger had left me a note, saying that he was going to Igor's apartment for a while to play video games. He also was a huge fan of video games, just as much as Igor was, so it did not surprise me at all. I still had not found a job yet, and I needed the money to pay for the class I was planning to take the next month. I could not call my father to help me with that because I knew that it was going to be hard on him, especially at that time of the month, knowing that he was saving for my fall tuition. I just needed to find a job, the sooner the better for me. Before I went to bed that night, I prayed to God and asked for his help as I always did. I particularly prayed that he remembered that he allowed me to come to the States and become a man for my family. Now, it was time for me to begin making that possible, I needed a job to become more independent and take care of myself, so my father could focus on my siblings back home.

I almost cried while saying my prayer, and it was the first time I had ever felt myself so deep in addressing God. I recalled my father's advice, when he told me that I should always ask God for anything I wanted to do and believe that he never should abandon me. I needed to feel God's presence in my life that night, especially with the stressful situation I was going through.

When I woke up the next day, as I began to do cleanings in the apartment, my phone rang and I could not determine who it was. So, I picked up, and here it was a woman's voice, asking if I was still looking for a job. First, I did not know what to say, but then remembered my prayer the other night. God was answering my prayer. I told the lady; I surely was still looking for a job and that I was available to start anytime she wanted me to. She sounded excited about my answer too.

"Well, Frank, do you have a pen and a paper handy so I can give you the address for our location?"

"Yea, I have a pen and a paper." I searched in every corner of the room where I had lately seen a pen and a paper. Finally, I grabbed one and told her to go ahead and spell the address for me.

"Well, Frank. First, where do you live?" she asked.

"I am by the Midway Mall on Texoma Parkway at the Hilltop Apartments."

"Wow! Frank, that sounds perfect, because we are just on Texoma Parkway too. You just should drive south, heading to Denison, and we will be just on your left. The name of our staffing service is Snelling. You cannot miss it. When do you think you could get here, Frank?"

"Well, I could head there even right now if you want to!"

"Great, Frank. In this case we will see in about an hour, giving you time to get yourself ready. Is that okay with you?"

"It is just perfect!" I spoke. "Thank you and see you later."

"Bye, Frank!"

I could not believe what I was experiencing that day. I had often been told that God listened to all our prayers every time we said them and that he would choose to answer them whenever he believed it was the right time for him, which was not in accordance with our time. But this time, it seemed to me that my time met God's time, and he decided to answer my prayer just when I needed it to happen. I sat down for a minute after I hung up the phone with the lady. Then, I began to thank God for his blessing and promised him that I was going to keep that job and work as hard as I could to please my supervisors. Then, I rushed to the shower to get myself ready and head to Snelling. I did not even have breakfast that morning, nor did I knock on Beranger's door to check if he made it home the other night.

Snelling was close to Hilltop, and in fact, I could walk there. When I got there, I was surprised to see one of the guys I had met at Grayson who lived at Hilltop too. His name was Younes Ballay. He was also from Gabon and had been to Grayson two semesters longer than me so he was about to be done, as normally one needed four semesters to complete most requirements for graduation.

"Hey man, what are you doing here?" I asked him.

"Well, I am the one who gave them your number, as I met Guy Patrick the other day at his job and he told me you were looking for a job. I work at this company and they've asked me to bring someone in because they've opened positions in a bakery not too far from here."

"Really!" I could not say much to thank Younes. I had met him just once and we did not spend enough time getting to know each other, and there he was, helping me get a job. Sometimes, it is when you expect it the least that you get what you need the most. Younes just proved it to me that day. It was not easy for one to tell that Younes was from Gabon. He was light skin, and that was because his father married a woman from Morocco and she was quite light skinned. I thought he was French when we first met at Mrs. Pearce's office. But then he started speaking like most Gabonese, using our own broken French words that only one from Gabon could know. Thus, I realized that he came from a bi-racial family. Younes had chosen to help me after Guy had told him about my situation. He could have thought of someone else, as he surely knew other friends whom he could have proposed the job to, but he chose me. To me, that was enough to consider him more than just a friend. I recalled those sermons I used to listen to at the Great Refuge Temple in New York. Pastor Lee Bonner always said that God uses people to bless other people and that is exactly what was happening to Younes and me.

We stood in a room, which was a waiting room for most people who came in and waited to be called into one of three office desks held by three nice-looking ladies. They were holding interviews, and I just had to sit and wait for my name to be called. Younes was there to pick up his paycheck, so he could not stay with me any longer. I told him I was going to be all right and that I would let him know how it went whenever I was done. He waved at one of the ladies who waved back to him with a large smile as though saying, "Thank you, Younes." I said to myself that certainly she was the one who gave me the call that morning and before I was even done thinking so, she called, "Frank!"

I got up from my seat, answered "Yes," and walked toward her desk.

"How are you today, Frank? I am Amanda and I am the one who called you this morning."

"Hello, Amanda!"

"Well, you are a friend of Younes?" she asked.

"Yea, we come from the same country and we both attend Grayson County College."

"Okay, that sounds good. Well, Younes has been here with us for a while now. He is a nice guy and we all like him here. So, when he recommended you, we wanted to offer this opportunity to you and see how you can oversee the job." She said it with a very cool sense of humor, which made me smile for a moment before I could positively confirm the suggestion.

"Oh! Yes! I definitely could assure you that I am a diligent man, and especially, I learn fast, which makes me the right person for any type of job as long as a training is provided to me."

"Well, Frank, we do have a position for you today and this is really good for you because you would be working in a bakery which is located on the other side of our building." She pointed outside and I could perceive the sign with the words "Yahoo Bakery" capitalized to get Texoma Highway drivers' attention. This was perfect, I said to myself. I will not even need to drive to work. Yahoo Bakery was just three blocks away from Red Lobster. This was God's working power in my life. Not only was he providing me with a job I needed so desperately, but he also was making sure I did not have any problem getting there, by making it easy to reach by just walking from home. For what else could someone ask God? He was showing me that if I asked him what I needed, he was going to bring it to me.

I told Amanda that I was ready to start working that very same day if she wanted me to. She smiled and hit me on the shoulder, telling one of her colleagues that I was the man they needed for Yahoo Bakery. Then, she asked for my entire name, address, and identification she needed to get me into her computer system, before she handed me a paper with the directions to Yahoo Bakery and the number of a woman named Courtney.

"Okay, Frank. Courtney is Manager at Yahoo Bakery. You need to get there tomorrow morning at six a.m., and make sure you get there on time, Frank. It is especially important that you be on time on your first day. You would tell her that you come from Snelling, and she would show you whatever they expect from you over there. Do you think you could be there at six a.m., Frank?"

I knew it was quite early, but I had already had to wake up earlier than that, so it was not going to be a major issue for me. I told her that I could do that.

"Okay, Frank, the other thing is that you need to have black shoes and a simple jean would be all right with a long-sleeve shirt, preferably. Other than that, you are good to go. You will be paid every other Thursday, and make sure that you have your supervisor sign these time sheets before you bring them back to us at the end of every week. We cannot pay you if you do not have the time sheet here on time and signed by your supervisor."

"Understood! Amanda, I would like to thank you again for this job, and you all have a good day then."

"Bye, Frank, and be on time tomorrow!" she said while I was leaving her desk.

As I walked back to my apartment, I could feel immense joy and satisfaction within myself. The stress was over, and all I had to do was to make it to Yahoo Bakery on time the next day. I was going to be able to pay for my English class without having to call my dad for help. I even began to plan to save money and paying for one half of the fall semester's tuition so that it would not be too hard on my father. Anyone who met me that day could tell that something good had happened to me. When I reached my apartment, Beranger was already up, fixing himself something to eat for breakfast.

"Hey, friend, what happened to you?" he asked when I entered the room.

"You will not believe this, man! I just got a job, and the good thing about it is that the job is on the other side of Texoma, which means that I do not need to get a ride to be to work."

"Wow! Bro, I am happy for you. God never forget his children, man!"

"Oh yes, man! He sure does not forget his children!"

I stayed home that day and did not want to go to look for another job as I had been doing every morning. Instead, I sat in the living room and thought about my life in general. I looked back to the time I was still in Gabon with my family. I thought about what life would have been for me had I not moved to the States. Certainly, I would still be living with my parents and depending on them for everything. I might have moved to the campus at Omar Bongo Ondimba University, as my classmates did after graduating, at least those who did not go abroad. I would not have to work to pay for my school, because it was not required to do so at Omar Bongo Ondimba University. One had only to enroll in a department and purchase their study materials, which varied depending on the instructor they had. I knew friends who attended university while I was still in high school, and sometimes I would visit them, as they stayed on campus. It felt so good to enter the huge gate at the campus's main entrance and begin imagining myself as a college student. They had their own restaurant, which could admit thousands and thousands of students. My friend Waldrys was in his first-year law program and he had a room on campus. He sometimes would call me and other friends to meet with him there on a Saturday night. We all would go out, having fun rolling from one club to the other all night long and finally returning to his room and sleeping there for hours, before waking up and thinking about what was next on Sunday night. We used to have non-stop parties those days, and the thing about it was that we always were the best students in our different classes. In fact, people had the idea that the more students went out and had fun, the less well they would do in class. This was not the case for us. We lived under a code, and it was all about the Martin Luther King, Jr. English Club of which we all were active members. Waldrys was the one who introduced me to the club as a senior at Gondjout High School. He had had his first experience with the English language while helping American Peace Corps volunteers who came to his village for projects. He served as a guide to them, and it was through one of the volunteers that he learned English. By the time he was a senior, Waldrys spoke English like an American. His accent was beautiful, and one could spend the entire day listening to him speak English. He was the President of the Club at that time and we met each other during one of the Club's opening campaigns on campus. I was still a sophomore when Waldrys came to my class to talk about the Martin Luther King, Jr. English Club. We were having a history class when he asked our instructor if he could come in to give a message to the class about the Club. The instructor agreed. He introduced himself in French and told us he was the president of the Martin Luther King, Jr. English Club. Partway through, the instructor stopped him and asked if he could give his message in English. Waldrys smiled and replied that he absolutely would do it in English. When he started to speak in English, I felt like something had grabbed me, as though I were possessed or something. The tone was loud, and his voice reached every corner of the room. I had never heard someone speak English before me like that in person. He sounded like an American reporter or journalist. He was eloquent and fluent. He was not even done speaking yet when the entire classroom gave him a round of applause to signify how amazed and impressed, we all were. I am quite sure that even the instructor that day could recognize that the guy was good. I waited for class to be over before heading to the Club's meeting building, which was not too far from my class. When I got there, there were other students standing outside and asking what it took to become an active member. I introduced myself to a guy whose first name was Davy, but he told me to call him Smith. It was his nickname. He revealed to me that he also was touched by Waldrys's presentation in his classroom hours earlier. I told him I could not miss this opportunity to go learn English with that guy. We both stood outside waiting as more students arrived to register for the Club. I did not know there were students at Gondjout High who were interested in studying English. After about an hour, Waldrys walked toward Smith and me.

"Hey, guys! How are you doing?"

I did not know English by that time, but I did remember how to respond to a how are-you type of question, so I said, "I am doing fine, and you?"

He replied by saying something I did not understand, but it was just so cool listen to him speak. Then, Smith responded by saying that he was Davy but liked to be called Smith. Waldrys said," Then, Hi, Mr. Smith! I hope you are excited to join the Club today!"

I was sure Smith understood well what Waldrys said to him because he smiled and nodded to agree with whatever Waldrys said to him. The whole situation made me want to join the Club even more than I wanted to. I just wanted to be around that guy all the time and pick up the language just as he did. Soon, Smith and I became constantly active members of the Club and we would even go around the campus and invite other students to join. We searched for new English expressions every day. Sometimes, we looked-for brand-new expressions to impress everyone else in the Club. By the end of the year, Smith and I could manage an entire English conversation with Waldrys with no need to use French to make sure we said something right. Waldrys was proud of how fast we picked up English and became just as fluent as he was. There were other guys who also became fluent as Smith and I had. There was Boris, Wally, who was my roommate and whose English improved amazingly fast, and Bastain, who we all labeled "the grammar boy" because of how good he had become at English grammar. He read English grammar every day and made sure that he understood every point that could cause trouble to even natives of the language. Other students grew to be just as good at English through the Club that year.

The day went by fast as I sat on the couch and recalled my days at the Club with my friends. Beranger was back from Igor's apartment, and I did not even see him coming in. I must have been asleep. I got up as the sun began to die down and decided to go for a run and relax outside. I needed to feel in decent shape for the next day at Yahoo Bakery. Hilltop was nice during the summer. You could see the sun disappearing from apartment roofs, and it looked beautiful as I ran around the complex, stopping sometimes to say hello to a friend sitting on the stairs of his apartment building and reading a book. Hilltop had become more like a student residence, as tenants were students at Grayson County College, so everybody knew everybody. I had gotten in the habit of going for a run most evenings, relaxing my mind while making sure I stayed in good physical health.

Early the next morning, I woke up, had my breakfast, and headed to Yahoo Bakery. It took me less than twenty minutes to walk to the job. The building looked small from the front entrance and appeared from the outside as shop rather than an actual bakery. It was a very spacious on the inside. There was a button at the front door, and the lady at Snelling had mentioned that I should push it and wait for someone to come open the door for me. After I pushed the button, a low male voice asked who that was. I responded by saying I was sent by Snelling and my name was Frank. The man told me to wait, as he would get me. Minutes later, the door was pushed open, and I saw a heavy Black man standing before me. He introduced himself and told me I could call him OB, and he was going to be my supervisor. I greeted the man back and told him he could call me Frank, as I was sure my last name was going to be an issue for him. We both joked a little bit about my name as we walked into a room almost filled with other people. Most employees at Yahoo Bakery were women, and they were from Mexico. They spoke only in Spanish. OB introduced me to another Black guy who had just come in the room and was putting his apron on. His name was Ronny, and he seemed like a nice guy. The three of us were the only males in the entire place to be working on the line. After everybody seemed to be ready to begin their shift, a white woman, whom I would say was in her forties, came in, and as soon as she entered the room, a deep silence followed. All the Mexican women in the room seemed to be afraid of the woman; one could tell that the woman had influence in the building. OB walked up to her, as she asked that he join her before the rest of us. She introduced herself as Connie, and she was the general manager of the bakery. She spoke with a strong and tough tone. She reminded me of Mrs. Gamba, who taught German at Gondjout High School. She would often say before we started class that, to speak German, we needed to make sure we ate and had energy because the language itself was a strong one. Connie gave orders and instruction about the way everyone should work on the line and make sure that all products were managed with care. Yahoo Bakery made cakes with a variety of flavors. Their products were sold at Walmart and other retailers in Texas. After she was done explaining everything about the company's rules and expectations, she asked if anybody had a question. No one had anything to say. I could tell that those Mexican women surely had things to ask, but the language barrier was an issue for them. Then, OB introduced me to Connie and told her I was the one sent by Snelling. Connie looked at me, and with the same tone she had while talking to the whole bakery, she asked if I had any baking experience. I told her I did not, but that I surely could learn fast. She smiled from the side and told me not to worry about it because OB would make sure I became a lead baker. OB laughed at that and I just smiled because I did not know if she was being nice to me or was just going to give another order. Then, she told me that she read my file from Snelling and noticed that I knew Spanish, too. I told her that I surely could express myself in Spanish if I needed to. This time, her facial expression changed; she was happy to hear that.

"At least I have someone who would help translate my orders here in the room. What do you think about that, Frank?" She asked me now with a very friendly voice.

"Well, I surely would not mind helping the company with my language skills."

"Good. From now on, you will be translating all that I say to the other employees, as I know they do not get me right all the time. And so far, thank you, Frank."

"That's fine, Connie!"

Then, OB hit my shoulder and handed a white apron to me with a hair-covering plastic he asked that I put on before we walked to the line, where everyone else already had headed. I felt privileged that day to be talking and laughing with Connie and OB while the other employees had left to begin their shift. Furthermore, it was on my first day at work. Usually, it took time in a company before one could hang around with the supervisor and general manager, especially one like Connie. I told myself that I surely was going to enjoy working at Yahoo Bakery. OB and Ronnie wore red aprons, which meant that they both either were supervisors or more experienced in the field; everyone else wore white aprons. As we walked to the line, OB showed me how things worked in the building. We walked around machines I had never seen before. I kept asking OB what they were for, and he gladly explained. Then, we went to a stairway, away from where everyone else worked. I said to myself, here is another privilege.

OB took me to another room where Ronnie and a Black woman I had not seen in the meeting room were working. They were decorating cakes and setting them on wheeled shelves they covered before sending to a huge fridge.

"This is what you are going to be doing for the moment, Frank. I do not know if you have done any cake-decorating before, but it is pretty easy."

"No, OB. But yes, I can do this!" I replied excitedly about what I was going to be doing for work. I thought this was going to be the easiest job ever.

I worked at Yahoo Bakery seven days a week, and I would admit that although the job only paid minimum wage, I liked what I was doing, especially when I was sent to run the oven and make sure all cakes were baked at the right temperature with the right mixes. Everybody at Yahoo Bakery seemed to enjoy me. There were times when I would be singing while running the oven, dancing along with the songs I sang. It helped me focus on my job and not think about what time it was to get my break or get ready to leave as I saw employees do. I knew that OB and Mrs. Connie were pleased with my performance at work. I was always available for extra hours when needed. One morning, I remember, OB asked that I follow him to Mrs. Connie's office. I was a little anxious that day because anybody I had seen being called to Connie's office during working hours always came out with a not-too-good facial expression. I knew, though, that I did not do anything wrong; therefore, there should be nothing for me to worry about, but still, I could not help but wonder. Once in Connie's office, she stood up from her seat and walked toward me, asking how I was feeling that morning. I told her I was doing all right, as always. She smiled after I said that and then asked me if I knew the reason I was called into her office.

"No, I have no idea, Mrs. Connie."

"Well, Frank, I have called you to my office because I have noticed the excellent work you have been doing here since you were hired and I would even add that everybody likes you here. You make the day go by easily with your good humor, and I especially like that. I called Snelling this morning to stop your contract with them because I would like you to become a full-time employee of Yahoo Bakery if you like it. Here is a red apron for you to replace with the white one you have, as this symbolizes that you know what you are doing here and you do it well."

I frankly did not know what to say at first. I looked at OB and he just smiled and handed the apron to me. I was now going to wear a red apron, the same as Ronnie and OB, among every other employee.

"Thank you, Mrs. Connie, and yes, I appreciate working here, especially for the consideration and respect you show me. Thanks, again."

"All right, Frank, I would just need from you couple of papers to fill out and everything should be fine. Thanks, and you can go back to work then."

"Sure, Mrs. Connie." I walked out the office with a big smile on my face as I walked back towards the oven.

I could see the look on the face of the other employees, especially the Mexican women who had become like sisters and mothers to me. They all kept asking, "Franco, todo esta bien?"; they were asking if

176

everything was all right. I responded to them, "Si, si. Todo esta bien"; I reassured them that everything was okay.

As I continued working at Yahoo Bakery, I also enrolled for my summer class. I would go to work in the morning and then head to Grayson County College late in the evening to attend my class. The English 1301 class was fun and easier than I thought it would be, especially with Mrs. Patterson. We had to read texts from a huge book on American Literature. We were also required to draft essays on writing elements we studied in class. Mrs. Patterson was in fact nothing different from all Murielle had told me about her. She was straight in her remarks every time she had to grade papers. She really did not look over my paper because I was not a native in the language. Instead, I thought she was harder on my paper than the rest of my classmates. One day, she asked that everyone choose a poem to work on and make a presentation before the entire class. I chose a poem by Emily Dickinson, and the title of the poem was "The Heart is the Capital of the Mind." I researched the poem and used all the elements she required that we use when studying our poems. The day of my presentation, I wore a suit and looked neat, which was not common in the class. She complimented my dress and told me she liked students who dressed up for their presentation and that she was sure I had done an excellent job. As I presented my poem before my classmates, explaining all that I could of Emily Dickinson's poem, she kept insisting that I bring up more details because she did not believe I had searched it enough. I reassured her that I indeed worked on the poem enough to discuss it. At the end of the session, she asked that I stay for a minute after everyone else was gone. Then, she came to me and said, "I know that you might have felt a little embarrassed when I was picking on you during your presentation. But you should understand that usually when I pick on a student, it is because I realize and believe that you can be great in what you do. You are an incredibly good student, especially for one whose English is not the first language. I have been impressed by your confidence and the way you fluently express yourself in front of your classmates. In the past, I have had a couple of foreign students in my class but let me tell you that they were not as good as you are, and it just tells me that you can do better."

"Thank you, Mrs. Patterson."

"Now, I just want you to bring a little more work to your texts and research, especially about the authors so you could be more expressive in your presentation, okay?"

"Okay, Mrs. Patterson."

"You can leave now and see you next week."

"Bye."

I left the room that night with my spirit more boosted than ever. I knew that Mrs. Patterson was right and that I could in fact do better in my class. I promised myself to work harder on my reading and writing and pass the class with a better grade, which I later did, earning an A.

Summer was over, and everyone was getting ready for the next semester. I had not talked to my father for a long time then. I decided to give him a call and remind him of my tuition for the semester. I had been saving money from my work at Yahoo Bakery, but the truth was that, with a minimum wage paycheck, I honestly could not save money as I needed to pay my bills and my tuition. I needed help to be able to take those classes. I called my father and asked first how everybody was doing at home. He told me that all was fine and despite the same everyday struggles, they were doing all right. Then, I told him about the beginning of classes and that I needed his help to pay for tuition. My father did not need to say much for me to read his feelings because I had lived with him long enough to listen to his silence. I could tell that things were not all fine for him over there. Then, he asked whether I was going to go back to the dorm or stay off campus. I told him I believed that he could save more money with me living off campus than if I went back to the dorm. I told him

I had found a job that allowed me to afford my monthly expenses and that if he could just pay for my tuition, it would help me.

"Okay. I hear you, son. We will see what God will provide for us so we could take care of that."

"All right, Dad. I know he is going to help, so let us say that you will send me an email whenever you are ready then."

"Okay. Son, I sure will let you know. Take care of yourself, and always pray to your God."

"Bye, Dad."

"Bye."

That is how short the conversations with my father over the phone were. We could talk about what was important, and that was it. I would talk with my mother sometimes, but it was other types of conversations; just like most women, she would make sure we talked about every single detail about everything. She would always remind me how much she missed me and how my sisters bothered her about buying new clothes for them. Finally, she would ask if I already had a girlfriend and if I liked her and things like that, which did not embarrass me, because I had always been incredibly open with my mother. We used to talk about everything when I was still home. She was more like my sister than my mother, making it simpler.

After a couple of weeks had passed, my father sent me an email with references for a Western Union transaction he was able to make for me. I sent him a thank you reply as I got the numbers. Then, I realized that the amount of money my father had sent was not going to cover all my tuition fees. I could not ask him for more, because I knew that he could not do more if he had sent that amount. I felt sorry for my father because how hard it was for him to take care of all of us at the same time. I did not have any other money to add to what he had sent me to cover all the tuition. I thought about not taking classes as I had to take that semester, but I really did not have options. Immigration required for international student to take no less than twelve credit hours every single semester and maintain a certain GPA; the latter was not too much of an issue for me. I thought I should talk to someone who had been to Grayson County College a little longer to understand how things could be worked out in such situations. Guy Patrick seemed to be the one I needed to talk to. So, I went to his workplace, as it was quite okay for him to have visits in the store, he worked in. He was always in decent shape every time I met with him. One could not really tell when Guy Patrick had a problem or when he did not. Friends in the community gave him the nickname of "Wise Man."

"So, my brother, how are you doing today?" he asked as I entered the store.

"Oh, man! I am doing not too well today."

"Okay. What is disturbing your inner peace, brother?" he asked with his smile.

"Well, man, school is about to start and I am facing money issues to pay for all my tuition. I do not know what to do, man." I told him about the money my father sent me and how it was not going to cover the entire tuition amount.

"Yea. Brother, I am going through the very same trouble right now. I do not have all the money I need and we have just a week before classes begin."

I felt a little relieved to find out that I was not the only one having this kind of problem, but that did not mean that it pleased me to find out that Guy Patrick also had the same issue.

"What could we really do about it, man?" I asked him, still very anxious.

"Well, I have heard that there is something called facts, which would allow you to make down payments for your tuition and finish the payment following a specific deadline."

"Really?" I asked while trying to make sure he knew what he was talking about.

"Yea. You could read about it on the school's website. You do not even have to go to the registrar on campus for it. You need to have a bank account and a certain percentage of money they will require you pay first. After that, they will be taking the money from your account on due dates, but you can attend classes."

"Man! You do not even realize how much you are helping me right now with what you are telling me. I am going to check on it right away and figure out how to go through that."

"No problem, my brother. If you can get it done, please let me know so I could do the same by this weekend. Okay?" he asked.

"Sure, brother. I would let you know. Have good day at work now and do not work too hard as they say it!"

"Bye, Frank."

The information Guy Patrick gave me changed the mood of my day, and I headed straight to my computer at home to find out about the fact's method of payment. If this were possible, I believed I could be able to pay for the rest of my tuition. Especially with my job at Yahoo, I could just take money from each of my paychecks to complete my payments and have no more problems with tuition money for the coming semesters. To me, it looked more like a way to help my father, by being able to afford my education by myself. If he were not going to have to save money for my tuition, he could use the money to help my siblings at home or advance his personal projects. Thinking about it brought a smile to my face because I could already feel my father's pride when he would find out that I now could pay for my own school and by being able to do so, he could then take care of other things. After I got home and checked on the fact's payment plan, I found out that it came to be just as Guy Patrick had told me. I hurried to register and made the deposit required to begin the payment plan and to register for my classes. The next thing I had to do after I secured my payment and received the confirmation number for my transaction was to give Guy Patrick a call and let him know that he could in fact register via facts payment and make his deposit so he wouldn't have to worry about having to pay the full amount of his tuition. Since he still was at work, I left him a message so he could get it whenever his shift was done. All the money my father had sent for the tuition helped secure my payment plan and I was thankful for it, although I still was going to pay for the remaining balance. As time passed by and the semester started, my vision of life also began to get deeper and deeper. Everything made more sense to me, and instead of stressing out whenever difficulties arose or situations that before would have caused me to call my father for help, I kept control of my mind and looked carefully at what the purpose for all this was, seeking a solution for the problem on my own. I was beginning to develop a self-efficient mentality, which was a definite faculty for all men to develop as we went along with life. I no more would rush to ask for someone's help, until I had tried and tried in vain to solve the problem by myself. Not every single one of my attempts to solve my problems was effective, but at least I was beginning to take control of my life. I was then twenty-four years old, and I already realized that in America, at that age, most young men lived on their own, and seemed to have their lives figured out. I came from a different culture that saw nothing wrong for a grown man to remain at his parents' home. There was absolutely nothing morally or culturally wrong for a man to stay under his parents' care. I could not think like that anymore, as I began to realize that while in America, I was responsible for myself and nobody else was going to tackle my issues better than myself. My friendship with Guy Patrick also had to do with my transformation. Guy Patrick was the completion of that step I was beginning to take. I never saw Guy Patrick worrying about a problem, no matter how important or delicate the matter was. He always kept his mind strong and straight. One evening, after I was done with my classes, we met on campus and he asked if I could come to his place because he wanted to share something important with me. I told him I would not mind meeting him at his place. We drove to his place, which was not too far from the main campus and a few blocks from the Hilltop Village apartment complex. Guy had a roommate named Emmanuel. Emmanuel was originally from Cameroon, a neighbor country to Gabon on the northern border. He grew up in Gabon, and we all regarded him as Gabonese. He too had been attending Grayson County College, for about the same time Guy had been at Grayson. One other thing the three of us had in common, besides being students at Grayson County College and coming from Gabon, was our dialect. The three of us belonged to the same ethnic group, the Fang, whom you could find in Gabon and Cameroon. This brought us closer to each other, as we already shared that cultural origin. Emmanuel was done fixing diner by the time Guy and I got there. So, he suggested that I go to the kitchen and get something to eat before doing anything else. I gladly accepted his invitation, as did Guy Patrick. There was fried chicken mixed with a tomato sauce and other seasoning I could only recognize by taste, not name. Guy Patrick and I sat on a couch and enjoyed the delicious meal. After we were done eating, Guy Patrick asked that I follow him to his studying room, which was another room off the corner of the living room. As we got there, he turned on his computer and grabbed a USB key, which he proudly presented to me, saying, "This is my life, Frank." When I looked at the computer screen, it was about two hundred pages my friend had been writing.

"This is going to be my first book, Frank!" Guy Patrick said. "I am almost done with the editing part, although I still have about a few pages left."

"You know, Guy, I am not really surprised you've done such a work, man," I said while still containing my emotion while looking at Guy's writing. The title of the book was, "The Philosophy of Water," a book about finding inner happiness and gaining self-control. The book revealed absolutely the kind of person Guy Patrick was.

"You see, Frank, it is through those words that I express all my difficult moments. I try to do the best I can to live the principles I am teaching in this book. But that is not the whole point. In fact, I wanted you to see this project, which few know about, because I can feel the same force of inspiration and motivation within you. I don't know if you have ever thought of it some days, but I think you should consider beginning to write a book, my friend. Another thing I would like to add to you is that God does not give everything to everybody at the same time. What I mean is that there are people who have things that you may need or lack right now, but, if you look closer, you will see that he gave everyone talents and skills to use and develop so they could uplift themselves to the standard they wish to have. With your first book, or one of them, a best seller in this country, could you imagine how your life can change my friends? That is the reason I spend time on my book, to make sure I bring in ideas and words that truly would express the message I am conveying."

"Thank you so much, Guy! You do not even realize what you have brought into my heart now by allowing me to look at your writings. In fact, I had already thought about drafting a book, but as you know, in everything, one needs to have someone to look up to and make sure to resemble him. I had not found a peer whom I could relate to with such a project. I am now sure that the moment has come for me to begin thinking about writing in a more serious manner."

I could not stop staring at the screen and scrolling the mouse from one page to the other. Guy's words were so strong and deep in their meaning that at one point I thought I was reading some well-renowned expert in the domain of philosophy or self-improvement issues. Although Guy was not the first to talk to me about the necessity of drafting a book, because of the sorts of vibes they could get out of my person, he surely was one whom I really could look up to. As time went by and we barely had time to meet each other, Guy often asked if I had begun writing. He made sure to ask that question every single time we met, and it always sounded as a deep and important reminder within my spirit.

Things were going fine at Grayson County College. I already had been there for a year and a semester. I only had one semester left to graduate and move on to a four-year degree. I was still working at Yahoo Bakery, having more control over my working hours and my income. My father had been still helping me honor my payments via facts, so I could still register for my classes ahead of time and secure my seat for a class that was required for that time. It seemed to me that I had obtained the kind of peace of mind I was looking for and that certainly I had already learned what I needed to learn from life to move on to higher responsibilities and expectations. I was wrong, and soon, life was going to wake me up from that dream I had been in for months then, ignoring that nature had a unique way of bringing people back to earth when they had been flying high for a long time. Gravity still had to be applied in my life so that my faith and the things I had learned from past experiences would prove their just value.

I still remember that day when Mrs. Pearce called me to her office because there was a letter for me to pick up and that it seemed to her that the letter came from Gabon. I first could not understand what she was talking about because I did not see how I would receive a letter from Gabon when I could talk to parents whenever I needed to on the phone. When I got to her office, she handed me the letter and I could read my father's name on the return address. Why would my father mail a hand-written letter to me when he could just give me a call or email me? I asked myself. Certainly, the issue was a serious one. I decided to not open the letter until I got back to my apartment. Once home, I opened it and began reading the letter. It first began by my father reminding me that this was the first hand-written letter I was receiving from him since I had left home and that it should be deep in meaning to me. Then, he continued by giving news from the entire family and how every one of my siblings were doing. Finally, he came to the point by first asking that I always pray to God and be a strong-minded man and that I abstain myself from letting people know whenever I was going through difficult times, because I could only see people from their face, but could never know what was inside their heart, even when they were kind to me. That really sounded like my father; he always had a philosophical way of expressing his opinion on things one would say in more simplistic words. Then, he continued, saying that he was not sure he was going to be able to help me at all for the coming semester because he was going through hard financial times and there were so many things only, he could take care of. My twin sister was going to register in a private school that required payments every month. Another one of my brothers was going to take his baccalaureate exam that same year and needed to be put into private courses. Moreover, the grandparents back in the village kept getting sick, and one was required to go through an eye surgery or otherwise lose his sight – and all these were under my father's charge. As I continued reading the letter, I could feel tears shedding from my eyes along my cheeks. I felt so sorry for my father, to see how one man had to carry such a heavy load for the sake of his family and whom he represented in it. My father took care of every single member of our family, and the curious thing about it was that very few among those he took care of were grateful to him after they made it through and could live their own lives. The man did not have a life for himself. I do not even recall one single day in my childhood in which I had seen my father really enjoying the benefits of his hard work. He would sacrifice himself for both his family, his country, and not seem to get anything back in return that would allow him to have a decent life. When most medical doctors denied a particular assignment, my father went for it, despite how risky the assignment was. Sometimes, we believed at home that our father could even choose his work before his children, but that truly was not the case. The man was so dedicated to his work that he always wanted to do more than was required. We felt it was unfair that our father work that hard, especially in a country that did not even recognize him at his just value, but instead did anything to make his life miserable because of his neutral position in the country's politics. In summary, my father was informing me that he would not be able to financially support me, until he got everything back on track. After I read the letter, I dried my eyes, stretched a little, and began to think about what the letter really meant and how I was going to respond to the situation. I still had my job at Yahoo Bakery, even though I was not making enough money to entirely take care of my living expenses and my academic obligations. I also still could use the facts payment method to secure my registration for my last semester at Grayson County College. After I gathered all these elements together, I told myself that I did not have to worry about anything at all because I was going to be able to take care of myself as I had always done. It was the beginning of my last semester at Grayson. I had to take classes I had not taken previously that were required in order for me to graduate that semester. When I went to registrar's office to get the schedule of those classes, I found out that there was only one seat available for the class I needed to take and that if I did not secure that seat right away, I would have to wait until the next semester to take it. I could not miss that class and wait for another semester before graduating. Not only would I have had to pay more money for other classes because of the immigration obligation of twelve credits minimum, but also, one more semester meant that I would be a step behind everyone else I was supposed to graduate with. I could not allow that to happen. So, I rushed to the computer and opened the facts payment process page so I could make the payment right away. I had saved money for my rent and my other monthly bills; I decided to use that money to make the deposit required for me to secure my seat for the class. Everything went fine after I finished the process and was confirmed for the class. I felt relieved for a while. The next thing for me to do was to print out the class's schedule so I could get an idea of what my hours were going to be. When I got the schedule, I saw that the class hours matched with my hours at Yahoo Bakery. That was not good at all for me. "No! No!" I said to myself. That was not going to be any good for me. I could not change my hours at Yahoo to a later shift because Yahoo only had a morning shift for the entire day, and I was the one running the main oven. They could not allow me to make any change in my schedule to match my class hours. I decided to call OB and hear what he had to say about it before thinking of other options, if there were any. OB said that he did not believe the company could allow me to do so unless they just let me go for my class and maybe I could reapply after school was over. How was I going to live at Hilltop Village and pay my bills without a job? It suddenly began to feel as if the whole sky was getting darker on the top of my head. I also did not want to miss the opportunity to graduate with my class, as I was supposed to. Thousands of thoughts began to flow through my head as to what I was going to do next. I had already secured my seat by using my rent money, which meant that I needed to find money to pay my rent and other expenses. My friend BG had already told me that he too was going through tough times and that he was going to need my help with some of his monthly expenses, and I had promised him I was going to help him, just as he had done when I was in need. I could not even look at the clock to see what time it was when sitting before the computer at Grayson. My father's letter was suddenly raising more issues than I had imagined. I had to decide based on what really was important to me. I always said that for nothing would I trade my academic goals, because with a better education, I could get the best jobs ever. Was I going to drop my class for my job at Yahoo? I decided not to even think about it. Very boldly, I just decided to quit my job and keep my class. I needed instead to begin looking for another job as soon as I could. I needed to look for an evening or night job to be able to take care of my expenses. In addition to all that I needed to financially take care of were my monthly payments for the fact's registration. The agreement said that I must make monthly payments on time; otherwise, I could be withdrawn from my classes and not be able to get any refund of my deposit. I suddenly felt like I was taking one huge step backwards. "Why do I have to go through those troubles when almost close to bringing about certain stability in my life?" I asked myself. I felt like being close to the end of a tunnel and suddenly being pushed back into it.

I needed to talk to someone about it and only Guy Patrick could help me figure out what to do at that point. I gave him a call to make sure he was going to be able to meet with me that day. Luckily for me, he was off that day and could meet at any time. I decided not to waste a moment and headed straight to his place.

"What is going on, Mr. Frank?" Guy Patrick asked as I entered the room.

"I don't even know how to begin telling you all this, man!"

"Well, I could tell that something was mattering with you when you called and I hope it's none to do with your classes, is it?"

"Actually, it has to do with my entire education and everything else man. First, I received a letter from my father today, a letter, which he hand-wrote and had it mailed to the campus. He explained to me that because of some financial hardships back home, he was not going to be able to help pay for my tuition this semester. But that was not too much of something I could not deal with. The big problem is that I must quit my job at Yahoo Bakery to be able to take that class I need to complete my credits and be able to graduate this semester, because the class hours match with my work hours, and I cannot miss this class.

"Are there other ways for you to take the class with another instructor at a different time?"

"That is the problem, Guy. They offer only one class this semester and if I do not take it, I would have to wait till next semester, and I will not be able to graduate. I cannot afford to have to wait for another semester to graduate. What if problems occur next semester? I just cannot do that, man."

"Wow, I see that it is a pretty tough situation you have going on, bro. The only thing I think you could do now is to look for another job, man. I do not know how you going to do this, but you got to find another job."

"That is the very reason I came to meet with you, man. I do not know if there is a way that you could get me hired at your place. I could do anything if I could get paid something to cover my bills, man. I do not know, anything I could do, you know that."

I still remember the feeling in my heart that day when talking to my friend Guy Patrick and trying to convince him how ready I was for any type of job if it could help me pay my bills and afford my payments. I could almost feel tears deep in my eyes. I just managed to hold them in, to not look that desperate before my friend, even though it really was the case. I believed that Guy Patrick could help me find another job. I did not know how he was going to do that, but something in me made me believe that he was the right and only person I could talk to.

"Okay, Mr. Frank. I cannot guarantee that I am going to find something for you to do where I work at, but I would talk to my boss and see what he thinks about it. But again, I hope you still believe in not letting yourself go down when troubles come in. You need to stand above the problems and look further. Tomorrow, I will give you a call after I talk to my boss and we will see what we can do."

"Thank you so much man. I really hope your boss can find something for me to do. Rent is coming, and all those bills, and I had to use my savings to secure the deposit for my class. You understand the reason I so much need to find another job now."

"Everything will be all right, Mr. Frank. God will help find a solution."

I said good-bye to Guy Patrick, as I did not want to stay for long. He walked me out and reassured me that he would give me a call the next day. It was one of those days in which you do not even realize the sun has gone, leaving place to a darker sky with few stars to lead the night. My mind still was not at rest. It seemed as if the day was just beginning for me. I sat on a bench as I reached the main entrance of Hilltop Village. I did not want to go straight home that night. I felt morally weak and even my body was giving up on me. "Why? Why? Why?" I kept asking. It was not fair at all.

Days later, Guy Patrick gave me a call and told me that I needed to go to the Snelling office because they had been trying to contact me for a position in a factory close to Hilltop Village. For a reason, they had lost my contact information, and since most African students knew each other at Grayson, they supposed Guy Patrick could reach me. I thanked Guy Patrick and rushed to the Snelling office. After I got there and learned about the position, they asked if I could start the very same day. I really did not want to go to work that very same day, but I thought if I did not do so, they might give someone else the position. So, I told them I could start that day. The job schedule required that I work from five p.m. to five a.m. the next day Monday to Thursday. It was a long shift, but at least I could go to class in the morning. I had not worked that long hours before, and I did not realize how bad it was going to be to work those hours and go to class. I needed the job, and again, God had responded to my prayers and so I thought I had no need to complain about it. Everything seemed to work fine, as I could go to that job and get few hours of sleep before heading to Grayson by eight a.m. I managed to make sure I got all my homework done after class was over because I knew I needed to go sleep once I left the campus and before heading to work. It was not easy at all, but I did not have a choice. Some nights at work, when I took my break and sat on a bench outside of the building, my thoughts would be back home as I imagined that by the time I was still working, my family was sleeping and when I would be done working, they would already be awake and finishing their day. It was so painful to me, especially thinking about other students from Gabon I knew who did not have to work and could enjoy either their studying or their sleep at a time I was trading my hours to be able to have a life. My parents were still alive, and I thought I was living the life of an orphan. Sometimes, I got upset with my father when having those thoughts, but I never expressed that anger to him because I understood he was not having a good time either. Then, I would look around me and realize that I was not the only one going through that kind of life in Sherman among my fellow students. There were other students who resided at Hilltop too, and whom I would see in the morning when I was returning home from work; they would tell me they too were returning from a long night shift. I would admit that after I found out that I was not the only one having to work at night and go to class in the morning, I began to complain less and instead considered it proof of my determination to become an independent man. Andre was another student whose life was not too different from mine. He was originally from Benin but grew up in Gabon where his family lived. He too had to work night shifts to be able to pay for his school and the rest of his expenses. We met at Hilltop Village on a morning I was heading to Grayson and he needed a ride. I had seen him before in the complex, but we never introduced each other. That morning, he told me he was late for his class, because he slept too long after a long night shift at his work. I asked him where he worked and how he managed to get there. He responded that he worked in Gainesville, Texas, in a company called Weber Aircraft. He too was sent by Snelling, and only the night shift could allow him to continue with his classes. We kept talking about his job at Weber Aircraft, and I told him about my job too and how difficult it was to combine with school. We both agreed that it was not at all easy, but also agreed that we did not have options. Andre was a good guy, and he reminded me a little of Guy Patrick in his motivating spirit. He would always talk to me about his ambitions and how he was going to send money back home so his brother could go to school there. It seemed to me that Andre thought more about his family than he did of himself. Everything was often about what he was going to do for his parents or his brothers. I even recall one time asking him what he was going to do for himself. He never actually got around to giving me an answer about that, always trying to change the subject whenever I tried to bring it up. I, on the other hand, would tell him about things that I was going to do, starting with myself and then eventually with my family, because I believed that if I was happy, there was no reason for my family not to be. I worked nights and went to school for about three months. The closer it got to the end of the semester, the busier I got with homework and tests, and the more I felt like I was not going to make it. There were mornings I fell asleep during class and could not get anything of what the instructor had been talking about. It all reflected on my grades, and I was not proud of my performance at all. I knew that I could do better than what I was doing then, but I did not have enough time to study as hard as I needed and wanted to. I still remember one morning as class was dismissing, my instructor asked that I stayed for a minute. He asked why my grades were not good when good class participation normally reflected good grades. I did not want to tell him about my job, because I knew he could not do anything about it, but I reassured him that I was going to study harder and improve my class results. I knew I could not do it with my job but what else could I really say to him. There were mornings I wanted to go to the library and join other students to study or have discussion after class, but I could not do it because I needed to go sleep to work later. I saw my education take second place to my job, and this consumed me from within. I needed to pass the class to graduate, but I was almost sure now that I was not going to pass that class with the kind of grades I was collecting. True, I was paying my bills and making my class payments, but I was losing my determination to succeed at school. I looked at my class work to study, or even read less and less. I even asked for extra hours at work, as if what I already had was not enough. My major interests were now getting a new car and purchasing a new TV for my apartment, things that were not of any interest to me before. The truth was that I was discouraged by everything and I was letting that whole situation take me over. One morning, as I was heading to class, my instructor sent me to Mrs. Pearce's office because he had dropped me from the class because of poor grades. At first, I did not seem to really worry about it because I had already lost interest and I just agreed to drop the class. When I got to Mrs. Pearce's office, she was upset when she saw me and began asking what was wrong with me. I did not know what to tell her because I knew that she certainly was already aware of the problems I was going through. In fact, nothing that could ever happen to one international student's life was hidden to Mrs. Pearce. She knew everything about anything as far as all international students were concerned, especially for all of us who lived at Hilltop Village. At times, we thought she had hired some students to make sure they would inform her about what was going on in everyone's lives. Then, she told me that because I was withdrawn from that class, I was going to lose my status and that this was going to be dangerous for my visa. I could be required to return home by law if I were out of status. After she mentioned that, I began to look at the whole situation differently and more seriously. I did not want and never wanted to lose my status and be forced to return home with nothing achieved. What was I going to tell my father? How would I even be able to look at him or any one of my brothers and sisters? "No, no," I told Mrs. Pearce.

"You know well that I did not want this to happen to me. I have always been a good student until things began to get hard on me, Mrs. Pearce."

"Yes, FT." She called me what she liked. "I know you are a good student and I believe that you can do great, but I don't understand the reason you let yourself go now."

Tears in my eyes began to shed, and I just could not restrain myself from crying before Mrs. Pearce. I could not really describe how I felt, but I knew that I could not help crying and expressing how troubled I was. Then, I asked her what I was going to do since I was dropped from the class. She told me that because the instructor had already dropped me out, law required her to put me out of status even though she did not want to do so.

"Why? Why do you have to put me out of status, Mrs. Pearce?" I asked her with a partly broken voice.

"I cannot do otherwise, FT. I must do it; otherwise, I would be the one to get into trouble if the immigration service found out that you were not in class while I maintained you as currently enrolled."

"But is there anything that we could do to solve this problem?"

"The only thing we could do is to apply for reinstatement after I have terminated your status. You would need to re-apply for it and pay the fees required and hope you would be approved for re-instatement. I would help you go through that process, but you would have to make sure this does not happen again, FT."

"Okay, Mrs. Pearce. But how certain are you that they would reinstate me and not ask that I return home?"

"Well, FT I am pretty certain that you would be approved because there is a time limit for a student to remain out of status and be able to be reinstated. After you have passed six months being out of status, you normally could not be approved for reinstatement anymore, but your case is different. You would be okay, FT."

"Thank you so much, Mrs. Pearce! Thank you, and I do not know how else I could thank you."

"FT, you could thank me enough by making sure that you do well with your studies. That is the only thing I ask from all of you. I know you can do it, so stay focused and see me next week to begin this process of reinstatement."

After I left Mrs. Pearce's office, I stood outside for a moment and considered heaven, asking what exactly the meaning was of all that I was going through. I could not find an answer to really help me understand what was going on in my life. I moved to the United States with a heart filled with great academic ambitions and desire for success. But did I really know what it meant to succeed in life? I was beginning to question the very motivation that allowed me to make it to the States. True, I was just a kid graduating from high school and proud to have the respect and consideration of his parents, especially his father who saw something worth investing in. There were other things that I really needed to learn before I could pursue my academic goals. I had made it to the States too early and needed to spend time growing the man within me first, or maybe I had made the wrong choice in deciding to come to America. All these questions were flowing through my mind as I leaned on a wall by Mrs. Pearce's office building. I needed to find answers for these questions to be able to keep pushing forward with my life; otherwise, I would not be able to make it. These were questions that I needed to answer myself with no one else's opinion. I decided to not go to work that day and instead take the time to think about my life and try to find answers to those questions I was asking myself. I made sure I called the Snelling office to let them know I could not make it to work because I did not feel well at all. They were understanding enough, allowing me to take the day off and be to work the next day. I thanked them for it and headed to Fairview Park. It was there I thought that I needed to be to create space in my mind and begin to think about the next steps I was going to take. I had heard of other parks in Sherman, but I had only been to Fairview Park and really enjoyed the fresh air over there and the green line of trees and flowers; the green space was relaxing for my mind. I could see children jumping around their playing grounds, Hispanics playing soccer, as they always did the few times I had been to Fairview, other college students playing volleyball on the other side of the soccer field, a few other people group-studying around the park's tables that surrounded some areas, and all the fun activities going on at Fairview helped one to find harmony within the soul. I needed to decide once for all as far as the way I was going to manage my life from that time. I had already reached the very bottom of my academic failure by being dropped from a class I needed to be able to graduate, and worse, I had lost my student status, which even though I was going to re-apply for it, meant that I had failed the promise I made to my father. I needed to start everything all over and make sure I did not let go of myself anymore. For a moment, as I kept talking to myself from within, I heard a voice deep inside of me, reminding me of a quote by Dr. Martin Luther King, Jr., a quote we used to talk about at the club with my fellows. It said that the true strength of a man laid in his ability to rise when all hopes for him to do so had disappeared. I felt as if the spirit of Dr. King, which we always believed was with us at the Club, was coming back to me and asking me to stand back on my feet and take control of my life. I began to feel so comfortable with myself that the idea of having lost my status did not matter anymore. I was almost certain that I was going to be approved for reinstatement and that I just needed to reset my goals and ambitions while in America. I needed to realize that I was not the same anymore and that all the hardships I was going through were not meant to destroy me but help me grow stronger and mature. I needed to be able to give someone advice based on my own experiences and until I could put myself back on track, I could not really help someone else who encountered those difficulties. The voice kept revealing to me the hidden lessons behind challenging times. Examples of great people today, who before they became successful, had to go through down moments in their lives, began to flow in my mind, reassuring me of the greater good beyond my difficulties. Sometimes in life, before you got closer to the doors of the heaven, you would need to go down to the doors of hell first. If it were not meant for me to succeed and make something of myself in this life, I would not have made it to America, I said to myself. Everything happens for a reason, and a good reason, one that too often, we cannot perceive until we have gone through the moment of pain. I was realizing at that moment that the difficulties I was going through aimed at developing a complete man within me and I needed to grasp that concept in order for me to begin walking the right path. Sometimes it only took changing one thing to make another thing better. For instance, for me to achieve the kind of awakening I experienced that day at Fairview Park that helped me have a different outlook on the sufferings and difficulties I was going through, I needed to go away for a while and make space to rethink my life and reset my goals.

Mrs. Pearce and I went through the reinstatement process with the immigration services, and after we submitted the form required for the case, she told me that I should be receiving a letter indicating whether I was approved or not within the next three to four months, but I needed to make sure that I remained in school. I assured her that I would and that I was going to make sure I did not jeopardize my education anymore because of financial problems. I was determined to overcome every financial obstacle that stood before my academic goals. It was those moments of hardship that allowed me to grow, and it was through that adversity that I today esteem myself able to manage any situation. Having to work overnight shifts and respond to class obligations the next morning surely would not be viewed by some as the epitome of hardship, but for a person coming from a different environment, one that did not effectively prepare him for such a turn at such a decisive moment of his life, it was a heavy load to carry, one that I needed to first understand the necessity of. I had to grow from my father's son to my father's man. Finding a job and keeping it became for me not only a necessity to pay for my school tuition and monthly expenses at my apartment at Hilltop Village, but also a necessity for my personal emulation. I could not focus on doing well in my studies just to satisfy my parents and keep the promise I made to my father. It became more than just that. I needed to succeed for my own legacy, one people would remember me for. America had opened my eyes and allowed me to look at life in a more realistic way. I could now look around me and appreciate the taste of demanding work to achieve one's objective. Just like a young eagle learns how to fly, I had learned how to be a man through moments of hardships and psychological breakdowns. After about four months, the letter from immigration services arrived, and I was approved for reinstatement. I knew from that moment that I was meant to succeed in America and do remarkable things. Oncemore God had whispered into my ear and I could hear his voice saying to me, "I sent you to America for a purpose higher than just doing well in school. Find it, and everything shall make more sense to you." I recalled my father's words each time I would complain about things being too hard for me to bear: "My God is a faithful God." He would never abandon you. I realized that the hardships that led to me lose my status and get it back was essential even for my spiritual growth. My ability to deal with hard issues built a keen sense of confidence in me. I decided to challenge myself for higher goals from then on. Not only was I determined to attend Harvard University and become an attorney in America, but I also was determined to use all my potential to change the lives of the people around me. I could not stay in Sherman, Texas anymore. I needed to go somewhere else and start everything all over. I needed to go somewhere different, a place where I could begin to fly higher and appreciate all that I had learned in Texas. The news came to me from home that I had an uncle who resided in Omaha, Nebraska and that he had been trying to reach me so that I could stay with him and help manage his business. Once again, things were working out to my advantage at a moment I really felt the need to leave Sherman, Texas. Uncle Bertrand owned a car dealership in Omaha, Nebraska, but spent much of his time in Gabon. He would come to the States for his business and stay for a couple of months and then return to Gabon. He told me that he needed someone to stay at his place while he was gone because he had been paying rent for an apartment, he almost did not live in. Plus, he added that it was going to help me focus more on my studies and not have to worry about any kind of monthly expenses. He also assured me that I could find a job that would not affect my study time. I could not miss that kind of opportunity. I looked at it as my God opening a door for me to enter and begin to experience new things in a different setting. My sojourn in Sherman, Texas was at its end. I accepted my uncle's invitation to move to Omaha. Before I left Sherman, the month that followed, I decided to hold a dinner at my apartment with my friends so that I could tell them I was leaving and seize the opportunity to say thanks to those who had been supportive during my entire stay at Sherman. The night after the dinner, I began to feel the exact kind of feeling I had the day I left Gabon. In Sherman, we had formed a huge family regardless of our different countries of origin, and when one of us was leaving, it felt as if I was losing a relative. I talked to my friend that night about the power of determination. I told them about the struggles I had gone through, that I realized that they were not meant to destroy me, but to make me stronger and ready to tackle and carry heavier loads. As foreign students in the USA, we experienced the same problems and worries, and therefore, one's advice for a certain situation would be of benefit for all of us. Guy Patrick stayed the night at my place after everyone else had left. He asked again if I had started the book, and I told him I was still thinking about it. He smiled after I told him so, then he made a serious facial expression and told me that I needed to draft the book; otherwise, I would regret it one day.

"I believe in you, brother." He told me. "I believe in you and I know that you are going to make your dreams come true."

As we both sat in the living room, I told Guy Patrick that I knew that our friendship was meant to happen and that he had been such a good friend and a brother to me during my entire stay at Sherman. I told him that he did not have to worry about that book because I was going to write it and he was going to be among the first people to receive a copy of it after I was completely done with it and it was available for readers. Guy surely deserved that from me. He had played a significant role in helping me change into the man I was becoming. I had looked up to him for the values and virtues I was acquiring to have more control over my life throughout my time in America, and in my overall life. We finished the cups of tea I had made for us before we began talking, and as I walked him outside to the parking lot where his car was parked, he gave me one of those strong hugs that almost called for tears as we both realized that we were standing in the middle of a road where each of us was going to take a different path. Certainly, we were going to meet again, but the uncertainty of when that was going to happen made it a little bit difficult for the two of us. He murmured words in our language, saying that I needed to be a man, and I told him I would. Then, Guy left and I stood there in the parking lot, staring as he drove away. "Thank you, Lord, for this friend," I looked up to the sky filled with shining stars, relaxed, and hopeful about my next adventure.

"Omaha, Nebraska"

"Our deepest fear is not that we are inadequate. Our deepest fear is that we are powerful beyond measure. It is our light, not our darkness that most frightens us. We ask ourselves, 'who am I to be brilliant, gorgeous, talented, fabulous?' Actually, who are you not to be? You are a child of God. Your playing small does not serve the world."

~ Marianne Williamson

Time had passed since I left Sherman, Texas. Life, overall, had not changed much, I would say. The routine of daily struggles and challenges remained, the same for most people around me. I personally could not have remained the same. In fact, everything about me changed after I moved to Omaha. I was able to draw a clearer vision of what I wanted my life to look like, and what I needed to do to get that vision to come true. I could no longer allow the shadow of hardships to define my future or my dream. Determination, confidence, and faith had become the basis of my motivation to succeed and live up to my purpose in this life. I decided to set time aside to work on this book and hold the promise to my friend Guy Patrick. The more I wrote, the more I reminded myself of where I came from, and why it was important to never give up, to never quit, no matter what happens. Looking back, I have no regrets, only a smile today and a sense of purpose in the destiny God has assigned to be. So long as I could use my story to serve as a guidepost, a moral and spiritual boost for anyone who reads this book or hears me out, I am serving my purpose as a life-long learner and a life-long teacher. At times, I thought about my high schoolmates, and friends at Grayson County College who, in no time were able to complete their associates, bachelors, and master's degrees, while I struggled to make means and survive decently in America. I pushed myself every year to save aside some money to afford a complete undisturbed semester, while continuing to carry the weight of a family left behind and counting on me for assistance. Just as iron sharpens iron, I stood determined, and strong remembering the words of my friend Guy Patrick, "always make sure to walk your own walk, it is not how fast you make it to the final lane, but how well you make it."

Starting anew in Omaha, Nebraska, meant that I needed to close the doors of the past, and let in the opportunities of the present. I had successfully transferred my earned credit hours from Grayson County College to Metropolitan Community College towards an associate degree in international business, and I finally had managed to secure a working schedule that accommodated my time to study. I felt more confident with myself, and that was all that truly mattered for me to achieve my goals. Often, I would think of my friend Guy Patrick and his words of wisdom to uplift my spirit whenever I felt depressed; "You should never underestimate God's plans, Frank, because he already has planned your life," he would say.

So far, I had been quite satisfied and pleased with my life in Omaha. I looked around me every day and I saw people I did not know and people who did not know me. I felt the need to tell them about me, and it sent me straight to my book, which I felt to be, the most authentic way for me to become vulnerable with no fear and talk about myself. Determination has its place in the pursuit of happiness. Determination has its place in what I have become and for the next chapters of my journey in this life.

To you, my reader, I profoundly hope for this book to make you smile, because life is beautiful even with its painful moments. Stand up for your dream. There are setbacks, and challenging times along the way to your purpose, and they are parts of the journey, and they serve their purpose in your growth process. You need to learn to keep your eyes focused on the other end of the tunnel and learn from your mistakes. Truly, there is a purpose for everything that is happening in your life today, and it is not always meant to annihilate you. At all times, think positively, and smile at those who tell you that you will not make it, because you know you will. Too often, it is said that in the end, it is your destination that matters, I honestly believe, it is the experience of the journey that matters the most. Indeed, when you begin to acknowledge every moment as a part of something bigger in your life, good or bad, even your perception of destination changes.

A few Weeks after I arrived in Omaha, I got a job at a car wash facility, and one day during a conversation with a co-worker who asked about my goals and how I viewed my future in life, I replied that I planned on finishing college up to a doctorate degree, own my own business and make a difference in my home country Gabon. I further, added, that I also wanted to one day attend Harvard University, to walk the path of my greatest role models. Interestingly, but not surprisingly, in a sort of mocking tone, my co-worker replied that he did not believe any of that could happen for someone working at a car wash. I firmly looked at my co-worker, and replied that, even the biggest man in the world was once a baby, and all it took for someone to achieve their goal is the amount of determination, and commitment they put toward achieving that goal, no matter the sound of their job title at the moment.

By the time this book is published, I would hope that my co-worker, and friend at the car- wash had changed his perception of what is achievable or not in this life, especially when there is a will, a determination, and a commitment to do so. These few years in America have remarkably changed my outlook of life in a way I could not have imagined; I have become more aware of my strengths and weaknesses, but I have become more confident in the prospect of better days ahead. I stand before a mirror, feeling proud of the man I see. My father's words that night at the airport, more than ever, have become plain. In just years, away in America, I have grown from my father's son to my father's man.

I leave you with words of encouragement, a story to share with your family and friends, this book, as my long letter to the world. You are indeed the mastermind of what you want your life to be. Learn from your mistake, learn, and learn again. Be kind, and be good to people, it always comes back to you. Life is a conflict, and you must face it. Life is a fight, and you must engage in it, whether you want to or not. It takes a giant to race against giants, and this episode of my life that started as a foreign student in America, stirred up my determination to become a giant, and begin to stand for my dream.